EXPLORING

Arabic

Hisham Khalek

Joan G. Sheeran

EMC Publishing

ST. PAUL • LOS ANGELES • INDIANAPOLIS

rial Director: Alejandro Vargas

elopmental Editor: Diana Moen

duction Editor: Bob Dreas

Production Specialist: Macmillan Publishing Solutions

Cover Designer: Leslie Anderson

Illustrations: Lachina Publishing, Rolin Graphics

has been taken to verify the accuracy of information presented in this book. However, the authors, editors, and publisher
not accept responsibility for Web, e-mail, newsgroup, or chat room subject matter or content, or for consequences from
lication of the information in this book, and make no warranty, expressed or implied, with respect to its content.

hoto Credits

Assaad, Fadi/Reuters/Corbis: 188 (top and bottom), 192

nold, Bernd: 93 (top)

Archive, The/Corbis: 50 (left)

lantide Phototravel/Corbis: 46

éjar Latonda, Mónica: 61

urgess, Michelle: 260

orbis Royalty-Free: 23, 24, 25, 105 (top right), 111, 203, 248 (left and right), 275

reative Commons: vii (top right)

rist, Bob/Corbis: 47 (top)

escortes/photocuisine/Corbis: 49 (right)

igital Stock: 37, 38, 235, 249

otosearch: 13

ried, Robert: 67 (top right), 89, 160

aillard, Eric/Reuters/Corbis: 52 (top)

arding, Robert/World Imagery/Corbis: 29

oppé, E.O./Corbis Sygma: 226 (top)

neu.net: 189

Stockphoto.com: 45 (bottom), 129

Stockphoto.com/Calev, Joseph: 127 (right); Croizer, Jacques: 193; Gesell, Ines: 50, Gleave, Nathan: 86; Killer, Kathye: 8; Kindler, Björn: 62; Morino, Juan: 207; Pawtowka, Edyta: 1 (left); Peacock, John: 123

ashi, Ed/Corbis: 52 (bottom)

Khalek, Hisham: viii (top left), 1 (right), 43, 55, 88 (top left), 115 (bottom left), 119 (bottom), 130 (top), 135, 225 (bottom), 261, 273

Kraft, Wolf: 174

Mahdi, Mazen/epa/Corbis: 183 (left)

Mohammed, Hamad/Reuters/Corbis: 187

Mounzer, Nabil/epa/Corbis: 186

North, Chris/Cordaiy Photo Library Ltd./Corbis: 53 (bottom)

Osborne, Christine/Corbis: 169

Pavlovsky, Jacques/Sigma/Corbis: 228

PhotoQuest: 36

Saudi Aramco World/PADIA: viii (bottom left and bottom right), 105 (bottom), 115 (top right), 118 (top and bottom), 119 (top), 127 (bottom), 130 (bottom), 131, 133, 137, 183 (right), 197, 225 (top and bottom), 253 (top), 271

Simson, David: vii (bottom left and bottom right), viii (top right), 8, 67 (top left), 74, 93 (bottom), 103 (top and bottom), 155, 163, 239 (top), 265, 270, 274

Sternberg, Will: 79

Tunisia Tourist Office: vii (top left), 48, 115 (top left), 253 (bottom)

Vdovin, Ivan/JAI/Corbis: 45 (top)

Vernier, Jean Bernard/Corbis: 226 (bottom)

Wheeler, Nik/Corbis: 54

Wood, Roger/Corbis: 49 (left), 50 (bottom)

We have made every effort to trace the ownership of all copyrighted material and to secure permission from copyright holders.
n the event of any question arising as to the use of any material, we will be pleased to make the necessary corrections in future
rintings. Thanks are due to the aforementioned authors, publishers, and agents for permission to use the materials indicated.

SBN 978-0-82193-881-2

2009 by EMC Publishing, LLC
75 Montreal Way
t. Paul, MN 55102
-mail: educate@emcp.com
Web site: www.emcp.com

rinted in the United States of America

7 16 15 14 13 12 11 10 09 08   1 2 3 4 5 6 7 8 9 10

Introduction

Congratulations on starting your exploration of Arabic! The official language of about 300 million people living in 22 countries located in the Middle East and North Africa, it is recognized as one of the official languages of the United Nations.

Arabic is a Semitic language, which means it is one of several languages from the same family that includes Aramaic, Assyrian, Modern Hebrew, and a few others. Arabic is different from English because it is written from right to left in a cursive (handwriting) style. There is no printed form of the language with capital letters and small letters like in English. It also has a different alphabet and uses Indian numbers (٠١٢٣٤٥٦٧٨٩). Arabic has 28 consonants, three of which also function as long vowels (ا ، و ، ي). The dots over the letters, which have been added over the centuries, will help you distinguish the letters (ب ، ت ، ث ، ن ، ي). In *Exploring Arabic* you will find a "pronunciation helper" that uses the English alphabet. This "Romanization" will help you pronounce the Arabic words correctly.

Lebanese singer Elissa was recognized at the World Music Awards.

The Arab world has made contributions to mathematics, astronomy, medicine, physics, chemistry, and philosophy. Arab traders provided a crucial link between Eastern products, such as silk and spices, and European markets. There is a long history of Arab contributions to literature. Poets and prose writers used to recite and relate their literature to kings and rulers as well to the masses in public places. Perhaps you have heard of *The Arabian Nights* which comes from this tradition. In *Exploring Arabic* you will be learning about some of the cultural contributions made by Arab people, specifically in art, music, and literature.

You may not be aware that we have words in English that come from Arabic, for example, admiral, algebra, almanac, ayatolla, azure, calico, candy, checkmate, chemistry, cipher, cotton, crimson, gazelle, giraffe, Islam, loofah, mohair, monsoon, mosque, Muslim, Rubaiyyat, safari, Sahara, spinach, sugar, zero. If you don't know what all these words mean, take a few minutes to look them up in the dictionary. How many of these words are linked to the topics in the preceding paragraph? What categories would you put the remaining words in?

Did you know that "chemistry" is an Arabic word?

Someday you might have the opportunity to travel to an Arab country, where you will find the people hospitable, helpful, and accommodating. Do not be surprised if you are invited to share a morning breakfast on the shores of Casablanca, asked to join a wedding party in Mount Lebanon, or offered a cup of dark tea in the highlands of Yemen. Parts of the ancient world will

rise up before you, whether at the ancient sites of Babylon in Iraq; at the Temple of Jupiter in Baal-beck, Lebanon; at the majestic pyramids of Giza in Egypt; or at the Roman ruins of Carthage in Tunisia. Then you will be glad that you have a foundation in Arabic.

The pyramids of Giza are the only remaining monuments of the Seven Wonders of the Ancient World.

There is a section toward the end of each unit with symbols. Each symbol represents a word or expression in Arabic. This learning method is called "Symtalk" (symbols + talking). You will be asked to "read" the sentences and then to engage in a directed dialogue with a partner or describe a scene. When you write sentences in this section, you will be talking about the characters shown below. You can refer back to this page as often as you like until you learn the names of all the characters.

Symtalk Characters

As you start your study of Arabic, remember to be curious and ask questions and to be open to practicing new sounds and sentence patterns. Someday you may use Arabic in a real-world setting, so it will have useful applications. Have fun with Arabic!

Table of Contents

التحية والسلام **attaHiyya wassalaam**
1 . . . . *Greetings and Expressions of Courtesy*   **1**

غرفة الصف ولوازمها ومصطلحاتها
ghurfatuS-Saff walawaazimuha wamuSTalaHaatuha
13 . . . . *Classroom Objects and Commands*   **2**

الأرقام **al'arqaam**
29 . . . . *Numbers*   **3**

الجغرافيا **ajjughraafia**
43 . . . . *Geography*   **4**

البيت **'albayt**
67 . . . . *House*   **5**

العائلة **al'aa'ila**
79 . . . . *Family*   **6**

الحيوانات **alHayawaanaat**
93 . . . . *Animals*   **7**

المهن **almihan**
105 . . . . *Occupations*   **8**

الطعام **aTTaʿaam**
115 . . . . *Food*   **9**

الفن **alfann**
127 . . . . *Art*   **10**

aljism waSSiHHa الجسم والصحة **11**
Body and Health 141

almalaabis الملابس **12**
Clothing 155

alwaqt wal'alwaan الوقت والألوان **13**
Time and Colors 169

almooseeqa الموسيقى **14**
Music 183

aTTaqs walfuSool الطقس والفصول **15**
Weather and Seasons 197

al'ayyaam washshuhoor الأيام والشهور **16**
Days and Months 211

al'adab الأدب **17**
Literature 225

arraaHa wal'istijmaam الراحة والاستجمام **18**
Leisure and Recreation 239

attasawwuq التسوّق **19**
Shopping 253

assafar wal-muwaaSalaat السفر والمواصلات **20**
Travel and Transportation 265

Exploring

Port El Kantaoui, a Tunisian tourist town on the Mediterranean

A marina in the Gulf of Bahrain

. . . language

A store sign

A bilingual stop sign

...people

Enjoying a meal with family

Getting together with friends at a local shop

...culture

Selling fresh bread in Iraq

A Syrian artist in his studio

The Arab World

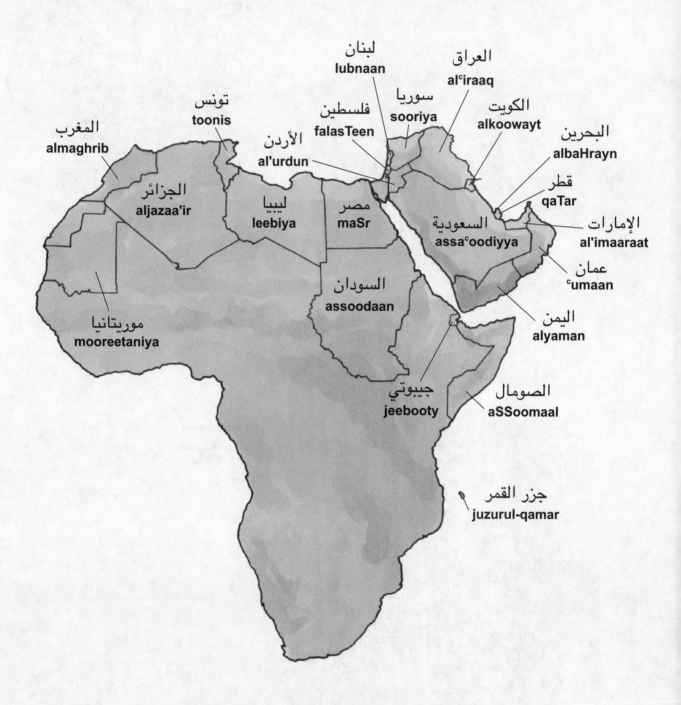

لبنان
lubnaan

العراق
al°iraaq

تونس
toonis

سوريا
sooriya

الكويت
alkoowayt

المغرب
almaghrib

فلسطين
falasTeen

البحرين
albaHrayn

الأردن
al'urdun

قطر
qaTar

الجزائر
aljazaa'ir

ليبيا
leebiya

مصر
maSr

الإمارات
al'imaaraat

السعودية
assa°oodiyya

عمان
°umaan

موريتانيا
mooreetaniya

السودان
assoodaan

اليمن
alyaman

جيبوتي
jeebooty

الصومال
aSSoomaal

جزر القمر
juzurul-qamar

Lebanon

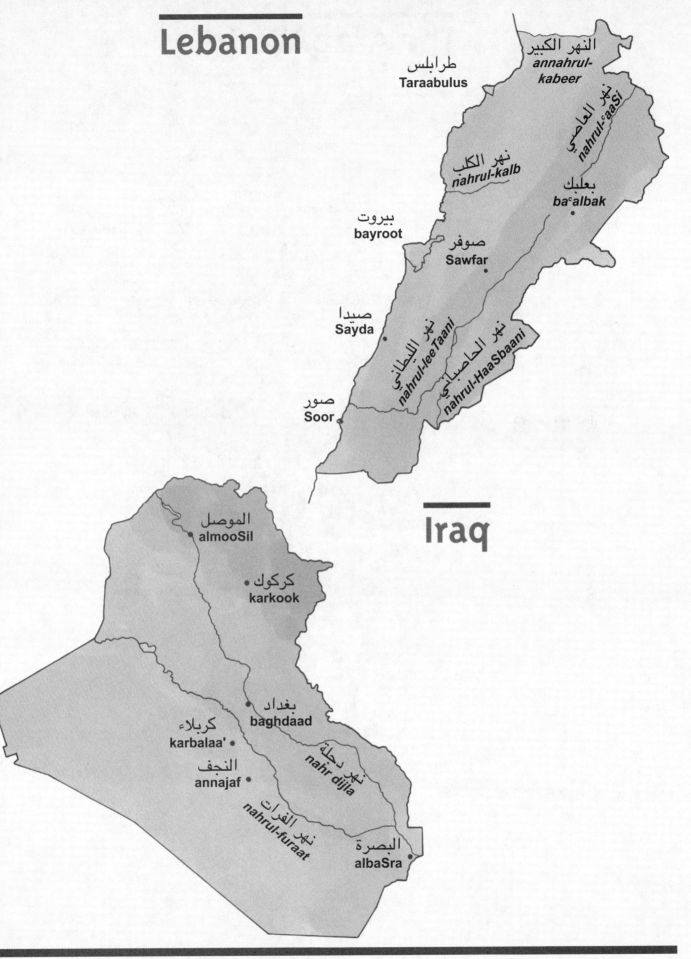

طرابلس
Taraabulus

النهر الكبير
annahrul-kabeer

نهر العاصي
nahrul-ªaaSi

نهر الكلب
nahrul-kalb

بعلبك
baªalbak

بيروت
bayroot

صوفر
Sawfar

صيدا
Sayda

نهر الليطاني
nahrul-leeTaani

نهر الحاصباني
nahrul-HaaSbaani

صور
Soor

Iraq

الموصل
almooSil

كركوك
karkook

بغداد
baghdaad

كربلاء
karbalaa'

دجلة
nahr dijla

النجف
annajaf

الفرات
nahrul-furaat

البصرة
albaSra

x

Unit 1

التحية والسلام

attaHiyya wassalaam
Greetings and Expressions of Courtesy

Vocabulary المفردات
almufradaat

Greetings attaHiyya wassalaam التحية والسلام

Peace be upon you. assalaamu ᶜalaykum السلام عليكم

صباح الخير
SabaaHul-khayr
Good morning.

نهاركم سعيد
nahaarukum saᶜeed
Good day./Good afternoon.

مساء الخير
masaa'ul-khayr
Good evening.

ليلة سعيدة
layla saᶜeeda
Good night.

Polite expressions 'adabiyyaat	أدبيات	
Please.	**min faDlak**	من فضلك
Thank you.	**shukran**	شكراً
You're welcome.	**ᶜafuwan**	عفواً
Excuse me.	**'aᶜdhurny**	أعذرني
I'm sorry.	**'aasif**	آسف

حظ سعيد
HaDH saᶜeed Good luck.

قليلاً
qaleelan
a little

نعم
naᶜam
Yes.

لا
la
No.

ما اسمكَ؟
ma- smuka?
What's your name?

اسمي جاد.
'ismi jaad.
My name is Jad.

تشرّفنا.
tasharrafna.
Nice to meet you.

كيف حالك؟
kayfa-Haaluk?
How are you?

بخير، الحمد لله، وأنتِ؟
bekhayr, alHamdulillaah, wa'anti?
Fine, thank God, and you?

هل تتكلّمين العربيّة؟
hal tatakallameenal-ᶜarabiyya?
Do you speak Arabic?

كويّس.
kuwayyis.
OK.

نعم أتكلّم العربية.
naᶜam 'atakallamul-ᶜarabiyya.
Yes. I speak Arabic.

- When you say "hello" to an adult, such as a teacher or a salesclerk, use the formal greeting: **assalamu ᶜalaykum.**
- **marHaba!** is an informal and casual greeting that is usually addressed to a friend: **marHaba ya, Ameera (f.)!**
- A girl says **tasharrafna!**: "It is an honor to meet you."
- Another expression is **ahlan wa sahlan!** It means "Welcome!"

Languages	lughaat	لغات
German	almaaniyyah	المانيّة
Arabic	alᶜarabiyya	العربيّة
Chinese	aSSeeniyya	الصينيّة
French	alfaransiyya	الفرنسيّة
English	al'ingleeziyya	الإنكليزيّة
Italian	al'itaaliyya	الإيطاليّة
Japanese	alyaabaaniyya	اليابانيّة
Portuguese	alburtughaaliyya	البرتغاليّة
Russian	arroosiyya	الروسيّة

هل تتكلّم الإنكليزية؟
hal tatakallamul-'ingleeziyya?
Do you speak English?

لا أتكلّم الإنكليزية.
la, atakallamul-'ingleeziyya.
No. I don't speak English.

مرحباً!
marHaban!
Hello! / Hi!

مع السلامة.
maᶜas- salaamah.
Good-bye.

إلى اللقاء.
'ilal-liqaa'.
See you later.

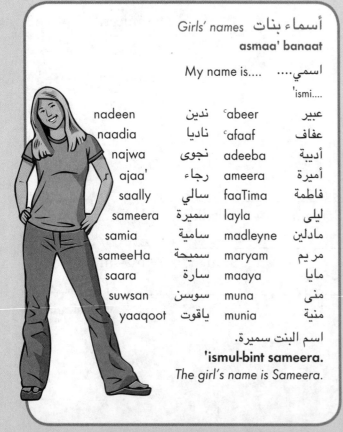

Girls' names أسماء بنات
asmaa' banaat

My name is.... اسمي....
'ismi....

nadeen	ندين	ᶜabeer	عبير
naadia	ناديا	ᶜafaaf	عفاف
najwa	نجوى	adeeba	أديبة
ajaa'	رجاء	ameera	أميرة
saally	سالي	faaTima	فاطمة
sameera	سميرة	layla	ليلى
samia	سامية	madleyne	مادلين
sameeHa	سميحة	maryam	مريم
saara	سارة	maaya	مايا
suwsan	سوسن	muna	منى
yaaqoot	ياقوت	munia	منية

اسم البنت سميرة.
'ismul-bint sameera.
The girl's name is Sameera.

Boys' names أسماء أولاد
asmaa' awlaad

My name is.... اسمي....
'ismi....

maHmood	محمود	ᶜimaad	عماد
makram	مكرم	adeeb	أديب
maalik	مالك	albert	ألبير
muHammad	محمد	anees	أنيس
qaySar	قيصر	baasim	باسم
raani	راني	faaris	فارس
saᶜeed	سعيد	ghassaan	غسان
talaal	طلال	ghaazi	غازي
tawfeeq	توفيق	jaad	جاد
tony	طوني	jood	جود
yoosuf	يوسف	juliaan	جوليان

اسم الولد جاد.
'ismul-walad jaad.
The boy's name is Jad.

Activities نشاطات

nashaaTaat

A Choose the word or expression that is different from the rest.

السلام عليكم	مرحباً	أهلاً وسهلاً	١. من فضلك
assalaamu ʿalaykum	marHaban	ahlan wasahlan	min faDlak
مع السلامة	المعذرة	إلى اللقاء	٢. ليلة سعيدة
maʿas salaama	almaʿdhara	ilal-liqaa'	layla saʿeeda
هل تتكلّم الفرنسيّة؟	كيف حالك؟	بخير الحمد لله	٣. كويّس
hal tatakallamul-faransiyya?	kayfa Haaluka?	bekhayr alHamdulillah	kuwayyis
آسف	نهاركم سعيد	صباح الخير	٤. مساء الخير
aasif	nahaarkum saʿeed	SabaaHul-khayr	masaa'ul-khayr
الألمانيّة	البرتغاليّة	العربيّة	٥. عفواً
al'almaaniyya	alburtughaaliyya	alʿarabiyya	ʿafuwan

B Circle the names belonging to girls.

nadeen ندين ٦.	maaya مايا ١.
saʿeed سعيد ٧.	sameera سميرة ٢.
jood جود ٨.	baasim باسم ٣.
ʿimaad عماد ٩.	jooliyaan جوليان ٤.
'adeeba أديبة ١٠.	munia منية ٥.

C In Arabic, write answers to the questions.

١. هل تتكلّم / تتكلّمين العربية؟ _____

hal tatakallam (*m.*) / tatakallameenal (*f.*) ʿarabiyya?

٢. ما اسمكَ / ما اسمك؟ _____

ma-smuka (*m.*) / ma-smuki (*f.*)?

٣. كيف الحال؟ _____

kayfal-Haal?

_____

_____

_____

_____

_____ .5

_____ .6

_____ .7

E **Write short answers in Arabic.**

1. How do you greet someone in the morning?

_____

2. How do you greet someone in the evening?

_____

3. What is customary to say after meeting someone?

_____

4. How do you wish someone good luck?

_____

5. Finish the following sentence:

أتكلّم (atakallam) _____.

F **Complete the dialogues in Arabic in writing.**

١. مايا (.f): مرحبا ، اسمي مايا وأنت؟
maaya: marHaba, 'ismi maaya wa'anta?
Maaya: Hello, my name is Maaya and you?

_____ :جوليان
jooliyaan:
Julian:

٢. باسم (.m): كيف الحال ندين؟
baasim: kayfal-Haal nadeen?
Baasim: How are you, Nadeen?

_____ :(.f) ندين
Nadeen:
Nadeen:

٣. رجاء (.f): هل تتكلّم العربيّة؟
rajaa': hal tatakallamul-ᶜarabiyya?
Rajaa, do you speak Arabic?

_____ :ألبير
albare:
Albert:

G لنتكلم! (*linatakallam!*) **Let's talk! Pretend you are meeting a classmate for the first time. Role-play a simple introduction.**

H دورك! (*dawrak!*) **It's your turn! What do you know in Arabic?**

1. Shake hands as you say hello to a friend.
2. Wave and say good-bye to a friend.
3. Name at least five boys' names and five girls' names.
4. Say that you speak English.

Proverb

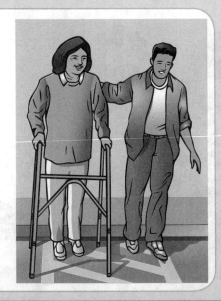

"الاحترام واجب.
al'iHtiraam waajib.
Respect is a duty."

How Do I Write the Arabic Alphabet?

alif ا and *baa* ب in the four different positions

Final	Medial	Initial	Independent
ـا	ـا	ا	ا
انا	مال	ارض	سمراء
Writing Practice			
ـا ـ	ـا ـ	ا	ا
انا	مال	ارض	سمراء

Final	Medial	Initial	Independent
ـب	ـبـ	بـ	ب
طيّب	لبن	بيت	باب
Writing Practice			
ـب	ـبـ	بـ	ب
طيّب	لبن	بيت	باب

Symtalk

I   In the space, write the correct word or expression in Arabic.

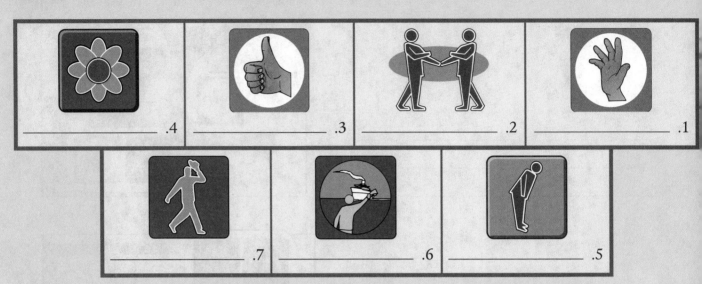

     4. _____   3. _____   2. _____   1. _____

     7. _____   6. _____   5. _____

J   Say the sentences; then write them in Arabic.

     3.   1.

_____   _____

_____   _____

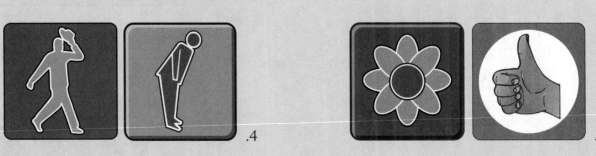

     4.   2.

_____   _____

_____   _____

Play the role of one of the characters in each scene. Then write the dialogue.

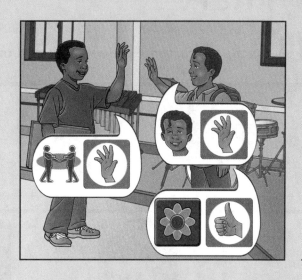

.1

_____
_____
_____

.2

_____
_____

.3

_____
_____

مساء الخير

صباح الخير

L **Look at the clippings to find the information requested below.**

1. What greeting can you find that you could use when you see your friends in the evening?

_____

2. Circle all the examples of the letters ا and ب on the clippings and write them below in the four different positions:

Final	Medial	Initial	Independent

Unit **2**

غرفة الصف ولوازمها ومصطلحاتها

ghurfatuS-Saff walawaazimuha wamuSTalaHaatuha

Classroom Objects and Commands

13

المفردات Vocabulary
almufradaat

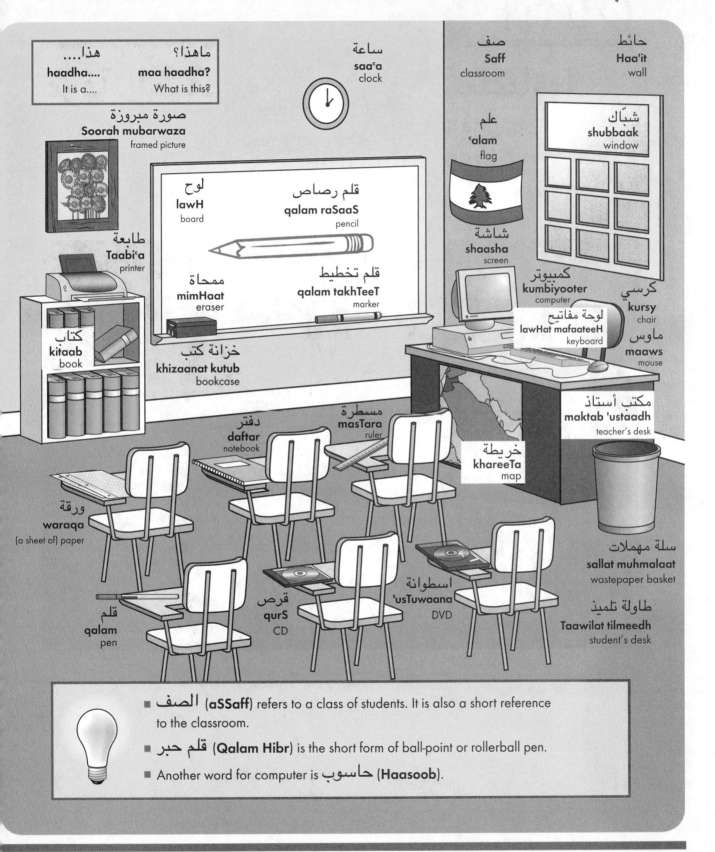

Arabic	Transliteration	English
هذا....	haadha....	It is a....
ماهذا؟	maa haadha?	What is this?
ساعة	saa‘a	clock
صف	Saff	classroom
حائط	Haa'it	wall
صورة مبروزة	Soorah mubarwaza	framed picture
علم	‘alam	flag
شبّاك	shubbaak	window
لوح	lawH	board
قلم رصاص	qalam raSaaS	pencil
طابعة	Taabi‘a	printer
شاشة	shaasha	screen
ممحاة	mimHaat	eraser
قلم تخطيط	qalam takhTeeT	marker
كتاب	kitaab	book
كمبيوتر	kumbiyooter	computer
كرسي	kursy	chair
لوحة مفاتيح	lawHat mafaateeH	keyboard
خزانة كتب	khizaanat kutub	bookcase
ماوس	maaws	mouse
دفتر	daftar	notebook
مسطرة	masTara	ruler
مكتب أستاذ	maktab 'ustaadh	teacher's desk
خريطة	khareeTa	map
ورقة	waraqa	(a sheet of) paper
سلة مهملات	sallat muhmalaat	wastepaper basket
قرص	qurS	CD
اسطوانة	'usTuwaana	DVD
طاولة تلميذ	Taawilat tilmeedh	student's desk
قلم	qalam	pen

- الصف (aSSaff) refers to a class of students. It is also a short reference to the classroom.
- قلم حبر (Qalam Hibr) is the short form of ball-point or rollerball pen.
- Another word for computer is حاسوب (Haasoob).

قل في العربية!
qul fil ʿarabiyya!
Say it in Arabic!

تكلّم!
takallam!
Speak!

أعد!
'aʿid!
Repeat!

أكتب!
'uktub!
Write!

أجب على السؤال!
'ajib ʿalas-su'aal!
Answer the question!

إذهب إلى اللوح!
'idhhab 'ilal-lawH!
Go to the board!

إرفع يدك!
'irfaʿ yadak!
Raise your hand!

أحضر ورقة!
'aHDir waraqa!
Take out a sheet of paper!

إفتح الكتاب!
'iftaH al-kitaab!
Open the book!

أغلق الكتاب!
'ughluq alkitaab!
Close the book!

إقرأ!
'iqra'a!
Read!

إستمع!
'istamiʿ!
Listen!

خطط وارسم!
khaTTiT warsum!
Make a sketch
(drawing, illustration)!

أكمل الجمل!
'akmil aljumal!
Complete the sentences!

إفتح الكمبيوتر!
'iftaH alkumbiyooter!
Turn the computer on!

أقفل الكمبيوتر!
'aqfil alkumbiyooter!
Turn the computer off!

Extra Vocabulary مفردات إضافيّة

mufradaat iDaafiyya

لإرسال فاكس **li'irsaal fax** to send a fax	لإرسال بريد **li'irsaal bareed** to send an e-mail	لبحث الموقع **libaHthil-mawqaʿ** to surf the Web
للطباعة **liTTibaaʿa** to print	للنسخ **linnaskh** to copy	للعب الفيديو **lilaʿibil video** to play a video game

Activities نشاطات

nashaaTaat

A Your teacher will say at random the words for 26 classroom objects in Arabic. After you hear the first word, find it in the list below and write "1" in the space provided. The second word you hear will be marked "2," and so on.

_____ ورقة waraqa	لوح lawH _____
_____ قلم تخطيط qalam takhTeeT	مسطرة masTara _____
_____ قلم رصاص qalam raSaaS	قرص qurS _____
_____ دفتر daftar	قلم qalam _____
_____ ماوس maaws	كتاب kitaab _____
_____ ساعة saaʿa	خريطة khareeTa _____
_____ خزانة كتب khizaanat kutub	سلة مهملات sallat muhmalaat _____
_____ ممحاة mimHaat	طابعة Taabiʿa _____
_____ شبّاك shubbaak	علم ʿalam _____
_____ شاشة shaasha	لوحة مفاتيح lawHat mafateeH _____
_____ طاولة تلميذ Taawilat tilmeedh	صورة Soora _____
_____ طاولة أستاذ Taawilat 'ustaadh	كرسي kursy _____
_____ اسطوانة 'usTuwaana	كمبيوتر kumbiyooter _____

B   **Answer these questions based on your own classroom.**

1. Do you have ورقة (*waraqa*) on your desk?

_____

2. Where is your علم (*ʿalam*)?

_____

3. How many شبّاك (*shubbaak*) does your room have?

_____

4. Is the طابعة (*Taabiʿa*) near the computer?

_____

5. Are there many كتب (*kutub*) in the خزانة الكتب (*khizaanatul kutub*)?

_____

C   **Write the name of each object in Arabic. Don't forget to connect the definite article الـ (*al*) to the noun.**

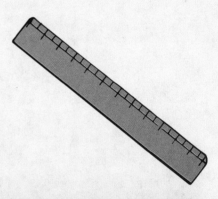

_____

_____

_____

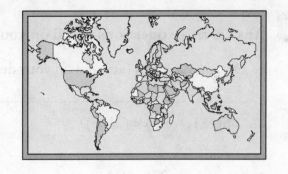

_____ .4

_____ .5

_____ .6

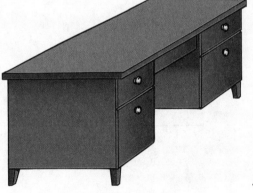

_____ .7

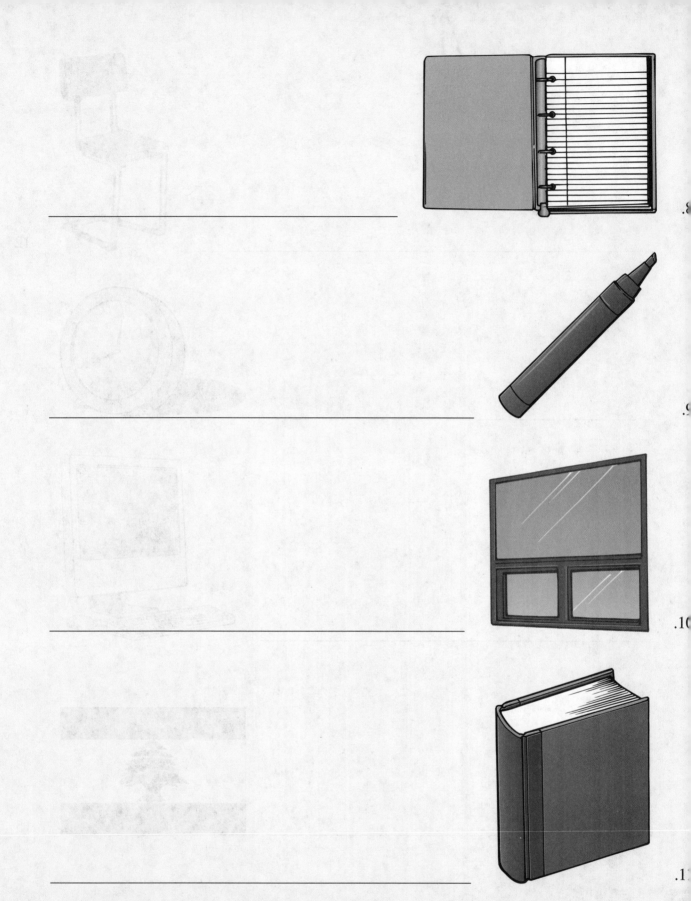

_____ 8.

_____ 9.

_____ 10.

_____ 11.

.12

_____

.13

_____

.14

_____

.15

_____

D **Complete the sentences.**

1. _____ هذا؟   3. هذا هوَ _____ كرسي.

2. _____ قلم.   4. هذا هوَ _____ كتاب.

E Do what your teacher commands.

F Write masculine and feminine commands in Arabic. (Feminine commands take a ي at the end of each word.)

	M.	F.	
1.	_____	_____	(Speak!)
2.	_____	_____	(Go to the board!)
3.	_____	_____	(Listen!)
4.	_____	_____	(Turn off the computer!)
5.	_____	_____	(Open the book!)

G Write a command in Arabic for each illustration.

_____

_____

3. _____

4. _____

5. _____

H لنتكلم! (*linatakallam!*) Point to a classroom object, such as a ruler. Ask:

هل هذه مسطرة؟
hal hadhihi masTara?

Your partner should answer:

نعم، هذه مسطرة.
naᶜam hadhihi masTara.

Point to a window. Ask:

هل هذا قلم؟
hal haadha qalam?

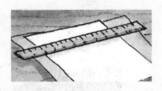

Your partner should answer

لا، هذا شبّاك.

laa, haadha shubbaak

Practice this pattern for ten classroom objects

I Word associations. You and your speaking partner should each make a list of five words or expressions from the classroom commands. Then say one of the words or expressions for your partner, who gives a word or expression that is related to what you said.

> مثال:
> mithaal:
> *Example:*
> A: يدك (yadak)
> B: إرفع (ʾirfaʿ)
>
> *or*
>
> B: إذهب (ʾidhhab)
> A: إلى اللوح (ʾilal-lawH)

J دورك! (*dawrak!*) With a partner, walk around your classroom. Point to ten different objects, asking your partner ما هذا / ما هذه؟ (*maa haadha / maa haadhihi*). If he / she answers incorrectly, change places. Now it is his / her turn to ask you the name of each item. Keep going until all ten objects have been correctly identified.

Proverb

رحلة الألف ميل تبدأ بخطوة **"**
riHlatul-'alf meel tabda' bikhaTwa
A one thousand mile journey
begins with one step. **"**

How Do I Write the Arabic Alphabet?

taa ت and *thaa* ث in the four different positions

Final	Medial	Initial	Independent
ت	ـتـ	تـ	ت
زيت	متر	تمر	مات
Writing Practice			
ـتـ	ـتـ	تـ	ت
زيت	متر	تمر	مات

Final	Medial	Initial	Independent
ث	ـثـ	ثـ	ث
عبث	عثر	ثوب	أثاث
Writing Practice			
ـثـ	ـثـ	ثـ	ث
عبث	عثر	ثوب	أثاث

Symtalk

K In the space or in your notebook, write the correct word or expression in Arabic.

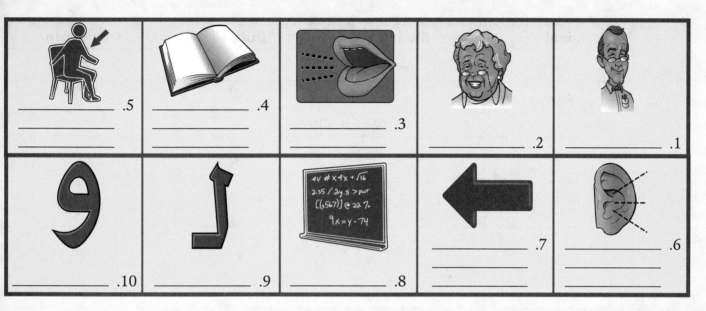

L Say the sentences, then write them in Arabic.

In Arabic, say and write a description of each scene.

_____

_____

_____

_____

.1

_____

_____

_____

_____

.2

_____

_____

_____

_____

.3

Living Language لغتنا الحيّة

lughatunal-Hayya

N **Look at the clippings to find the information requested below.**

1. Find the word that means "the class" and circle it. Then write it.

_____

2. Circle all the examples of the letters ت and ث in the clippings and write them below in the four different positions:

Final	Medial	Initial	Independent

Unit 3

الأرقام

al'arqaam

Numbers

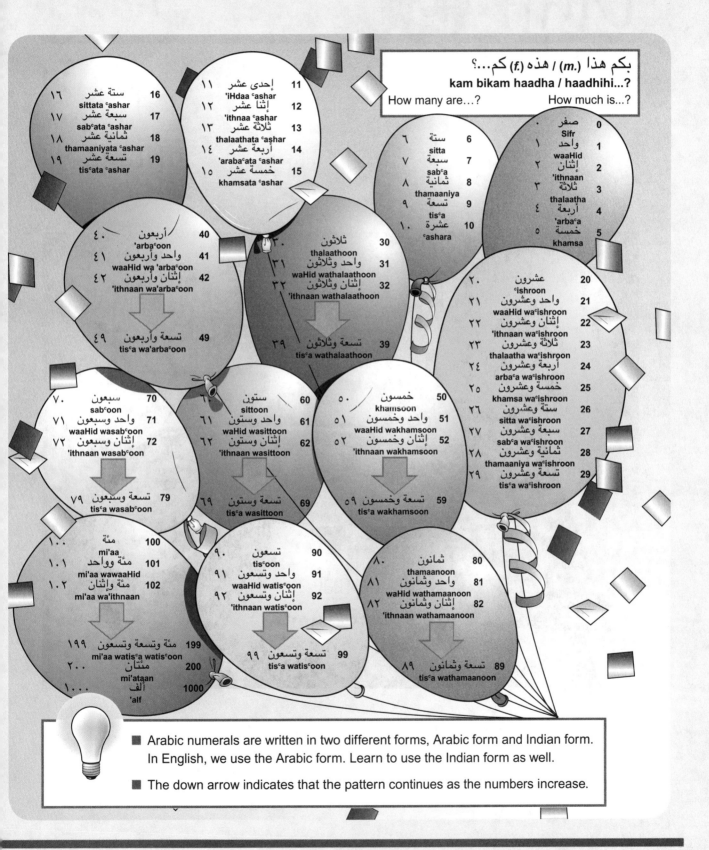

بكم هذا (m.) / هذه (f.) كم...؟
kam bikam haadha / haadhihi...?

How many are...?   How much is...?

صفر	Sifr	0
واحد	waaHid	1
إثنان	'ithnaan	2
ثلاثة	thalaatha	3
أربعة	'arba'a	4
خمسة	khamsa	5

ستة 16
sittata 'ashar
سبعة عشر 17
sab'ata 'ashar
ثمانية عشر 18
thamaaniyata 'ashar
تسعة عشر 19
tis'ata 'ashar

إحدى عشر 11
'iHdaa 'ashar
إثنا عشر 12
'ithnaa 'ashar
ثلاثة عشر 13
thalaathata 'ashar
أربعة عشر 14
'araba'ata 'ashar
خمسة عشر 15
khamsata 'ashar

ستة 6
sitta
سبعة 7
sab'a
ثمانية 8
thamaaniya
تسعة 9
tis'a
عشرة 10
'ashara

أربعون 40
'arba'oon
واحد وأربعون 41
waaHid wa 'arba'oon
إثنان وأربعون 42
'ithnaan wa'arba'oon

تسعة وأربعون 49
tis'a wa'arba'oon

ثلاثون 30
thalaathoon
واحد وثلاثون 31
waHid wathalaathoon
إثنان وثلاثون 32
'ithnaan wathalaathoon

تسعة وثلاثون 39
tis'a wathalaathoon

عشرون 20
'ishroon
واحد وعشرون 21
waaHid wa'ishroon
إثنان وعشرون 22
'ithnaan wa'ishroon
ثلاثة وعشرون 23
thalaatha wa'ishroon
أربعة وعشرون 24
arba'a wa'ishroon
خمسة وعشرون 25
khamsa wa'ishroon
ستة وعشرون 26
sitta wa'ishroon
سبعة وعشرون 27
sab'a wa'ishroon
ثمانية وعشرون 28
thamaaniya wa'ishroon
تسعة وعشرون 29
tis'a wa'ishroon

سبعون 70
sab'oon
واحد وسبعون 71
waaHid wasab'oon
إثنان وسبعون 72
'ithnaan wasab'oon

تسعة وسبعون 79
tis'a wasab'oon

ستون 60
sittoon
واحد وستون 61
waHid wasittoon
إثنان وستون 62
'ithnaan wasittoon

تسعة وستون 69
tis'a wasittoon

خمسون 50
khamsoon
واحد وخمسون 51
waaHid wakhamsoon
إثنان وخمسون 52
'ithnaan wakhamsoon

تسعة وخمسون 59
tis'a wakhamsoon

مئة 100
mi'aa
مئة وواحد 101
mi'aa wawaaHid
مئة وإثنان 102
mi'aa wa'ithnaan

مئة وتسعة وتسعون 199
mi'aa watis'a watis'oon
مئتان 200
mi'ataan
ألف 1000
'alf

تسعون 90
tis'oon
واحد وتسعون 91
waaHid watis'oon
إثنان وتسعون 92
'ithnaan watis'oon

تسعة وتسعون 99
tis'a watis'oon

ثمانون 80
thamaanoon
واحد وثمانون 81
waHid wathamaanoon
إثنان وثمانون 82
'ithnaan wathamaanoon

تسعة وثمانون 89
tis'a wathamaanoon

■ Arabic numerals are written in two different forms, Arabic form and Indian form. In English, we use the Arabic form. Learn to use the Indian form as well.

■ The down arrow indicates that the pattern continues as the numbers increase.

Extra Vocabulary مفردات إضافيّة

mufradaat iDaafiyya

واحد زائد إثنان يساوي كم؟
waHid zaa'id 'ithnaan yusaawi kam?
How much is two plus one?

يساوي ثلاثة.
yusaawi thalaatha.
That equals three.

الثمن aththaman the cost	
ثمنها thamanuha (*f.*) (it) costs	ثمنه thamanuhu (*m.*) (it) costs

بكم الكتاب؟
bikamil-kitaab?
How much does the book cost?

الكتاب بعشرة دولارات.
alkitaab bi'asharat doolaaraat.
The book costs ten dollars.

كم كتاب هناك؟
kam kitaab hunaaka?
How many notebooks are there?

هناك خمسة.
hunaaka khamsa.
There are five.

بكم؟
bikam?
How much?

كم؟
kam?
How many?

هل؟
hal?
Are there? Is there?

قسمة = ÷
qisma

ناقص = ━
naaqis

ضرب = ✕
Darb

زائد = +
zaa'id

Activities نشاطات

nashaaTaat

A After you have studied the numbers 1–10 and practiced saying them, try to write the numbers in Arabic from memory. في العربيّة من فضلك (*fil 'arabiyya min faDlak.*)

_____ .6		_____ 1.
_____ .7		_____ 2.
_____ .8		_____ 3.
_____ .9		_____ 4.
_____ .10		_____ 5.

B Rate yourself. How did you do? Circle your evaluation.

1. very well   2. fairly well   3. poorly

C Practice again. Identify the words by writing the corresponding Arabic numerals.

مثال:
mithaal:
Example:
إثنان <u>2</u>

4. تسعة (tisʿa) _____   1. خمسة (khamsa) _____

5. سبعة (sabʿa) _____   2. ثمانية (thamaaniya) _____

3. واحد (waaHid) _____

D Write the Arabic word for each number.

3. (6) _____   1. (3) _____

4. (10) _____   2. (4) _____

E Tell whether the following equations indicate addition, subtraction, multiplication, or division.

1. أربعة عشر قسمة سبعة يساوي إثنان.
arbaʿata ʿashar qisma sabʿa yusaawi 'ithnaan.

_____

2. إثنان زائد عشرة يساوي إثنا عشر.
'ithnaan zaa'id ʿashara yusaawi 'ithna ʿashar.

_____

3. ثمانية ضرب ثلاثة يساوي أربعة وعشرون.
thamaaniya Darb thalaatha yusaawi 'arbaʿa wa'ishroon.

_____

4. تسعة عشر ناقص ثلاثة عشر يساوي ستة.
tisʿata 'ashar naaqis thalaathata ʿashar yusaawi sitta.

_____

F Try once more to write out the Arabic words for numbers.
(*fil ʿarabiyya min faDlak.*) في العربية من فضلك)

6. (2) _____   1. (8) _____

7. (5) _____   2. (3) _____

8. (4) _____   3. (10) _____

9. (7) _____   4. (1) _____

10. (6) _____   5. (9) _____

G How many objects are in each group? Write out the Arabic numbers. Do not use numerals!

_____

_____

_____

_____

.5 _____

H How many objects are there all together?

_____

Now, write this sum in Arabic.

_____

I Write the answers to the math problems in Arabic.

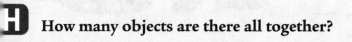

> مثال :
> mithaal:
> *Example:*
> ٤ — ٦ = إثنان
> 'ithnaan = 6 — 4
> 6 — 4 = *two*

.6 _____ = ١٠ + ٦٠	.1 _____ = ٤ × ١٢
.7 _____ = ١٥ — ٣٠	.2 _____ = ١٠ — ٣٠
.8 _____ = ٢ ÷ ٨٠	.3 _____ = ٦ — ٨
.9 _____ = ١٠ × ١٠	.4 _____ = ١٨ + ١٢
.10 _____ = ٤ + ١٥	.5 _____ = ٢ ÷ ١٠٠

J Your teacher will say ten numbers in Arabic. Write the corresponding Arabic numerals.

> **Example:** Teacher says: تسعة عشر *(tisᶜata ᶜashar)*
> You write: _____19_____

.6 _____	.1 _____
.7 _____	.2 _____
.8 _____	.3 _____
.9 _____	.4 _____
.10 _____	.5 _____

How many interior angles are there in each design? Circle the correct number.

أربعة (arbaʿa')   ثمانية (thamaaniya)

عشرة (ʿashara)   ثلاثة (thalaatha)

خمسة (khamsa)   ثلاثة (thalaatha)

أربعة (arbaʿa')   سبعة (sabʿa)

سبعة (sabʿa)   ستة (sitta)

إحدى عشر (iHdaa ʿashar')   خمسة (khamsa)

خمسة (khamsa)   تسعة (tisʿa)

ثمانية (thamaaniya)   إحدى عشر (iHdaa ʿashar')

L **Read the paragraph. Then choose the correct answers.**

هناك أشياء كثيرة في غرفة الصف. هناك واحد وعشرون كرسي
hunaaka 'ashyaa'a katheera fee ghurfatiS-Saff. hunaaka waaHid wa'ishroon kursy

وأربعة شبابيك وتسعة عشر دفتر وست محايات وخريطة.
wa'arba'at shabaabeek watis'at 'ashar daftar wa sitt maHHayaat wakhareeTa.

ثمن الكرسي واحد وسبعون دولاراً. وثمن الممحاة تسعون سنتاً.
thamanul-kursy waaHid wasab'oon doolaaran. wathamanul-mimHaat tis'oon santan.

و ثمن الخريطة ثمانون دولاراً.
wathamanul-khareeTa thamaanoon doolaaran.

cents **sant** سنت	dollars **doolaar** دولار

٤. كم دفتراً هناكَ؟
kam daftaran hunaaka?

أ. 91

ب. 25

ج. 19

د. 30

٥. كم شباكاً هناكَ؟
kam shubbakan hunaaka?

أ. 13

ب. 8

ج. 6

د. 4

١. هناكَ أَشياء _____ في غرفة الصف.
hunaaka 'ashyaa'... fee ghurfatuS-Saff.

أ. قليلة qaleela

ب. كثيرة katheera

ج. ألف alf

د. ثلاثة thalaatha

٢. مجموع الأشياء في الصف هو (.Add)
majmoo'ul-'ashyaa' fiS-Saff huwa

أ. واحد وأربعون waaHid wa'arba'oon

ب. ثمانية وخمسون thamaaniya wakhamsoon

ج. إثنان وعشرون 'ithnaan wa'ushroon

د. تسعون tis'oon

٣. بكم الكرسي؟
bikamil-kursy?

أ. $75

ب. $57

ج. $37

د. $73

M لنتكلم! (*linatakallam!*) Find out about prices. With your speaking partner, select six objects in the classroom. Ask your partner how much the first three cost. Then your partner should ask you about the remaining three items and you will answer.

مثال:
mithaal:
Example:

A: بكم القلم؟ bikamil-qalam?
B: بخمسة دولارات. bikhamsat doolaaraat.

N دورك! (*dawrak!*) With a classmate find out how many things are in your classroom. Look for these items: *kutub* كتب (books), *shabaabeek* شبابيك (windows), *dafaatir* دفاتر (notebooks), *'aqlaam* أقلام (pens), *kumbiyootaraat* كمبيوترات (computers), and *Taawilaat talaameedh* طاولات تلاميذ (student desks). After you have counted carefully, announce your findings to the class. Finally, add all the items to find out the total number of things you have. Write out the numbers on the board.

مثال:
mithaal:
Example:

A: كم كتاباً هناكَ؟
kam kitaaban hunaaka?
How many books are there?

B: هناكَ عشرون كتاباً.
hunaaka 'ishroon kitaaban.
There are twenty books.

Proverb

عصفور في اليد أحسن من عشرة على الشجرة

ᶜaSfoor fil-yadd 'aHsan min ᶜashara ᶜalash-shajara.

A bird in the hand is worth ten in the bush.

How Do I Write the Arabic Alphabet?

jeem ج , *Haa* ح , *khaa* خ in the four different positions

Final	Medial	Initial	Independent
ـج	ـجـ	جـ	ج
ثلج	عجيب	جمل	تاج
Writing Practice			
ـج	ـجـ	جـ	ج
ثلج	عجيب	جمل	تاج

Final	Medial	Initial	Independent
ـح	ـحـ	حـ	ح
ريح	بحر	حبيبي	تفاح
Writing Practice			
ـح	ـحـ	حـ	ح
ريح	بحر	حبيبي	تفاح

Final	Medial	Initial	Independent
ـخ	ـخـ	خـ	خ
فخ	تخت	خروف	خوخ
Writing Practice			
ـخ	ـخـ	خـ	خ
فخ	تخت	خروف	خوخ

Symtalk

O In the space, write the correct word or expression in Arabic.

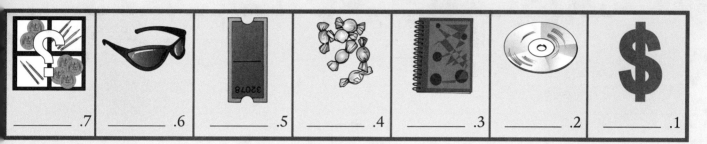

| .7 _____ | .6 _____ | .5 _____ | .4 _____ | .3 _____ | .2 _____ | .1 _____ |

P Say the sentences, then write them in Arabic.

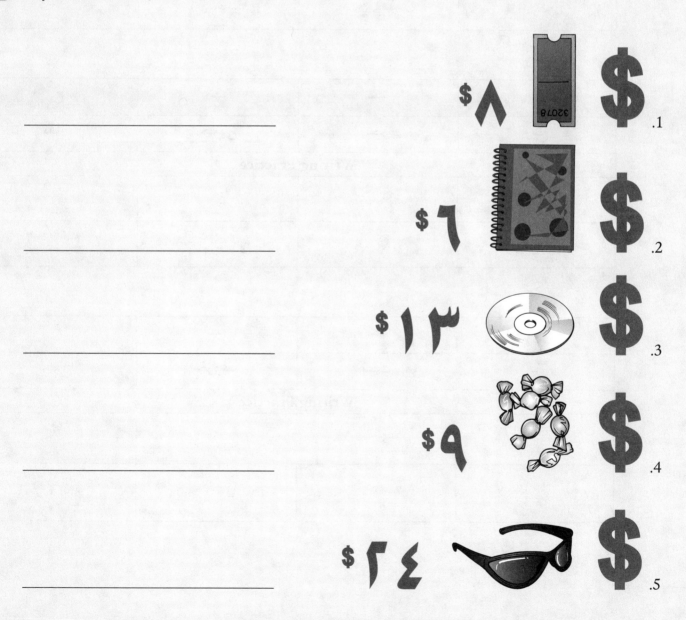

_____

_____

_____

_____

_____

Q Work with a partner. Ask the question or give the answer. Then, write the dialogue. Use lira ليرة in your answer.

> The "dinar" is used in Iraq. The "pound" is used in Lebanon.
> pound **lira** ليرة   dinar **deenar** دينار

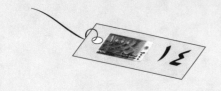

_____

_____

_____

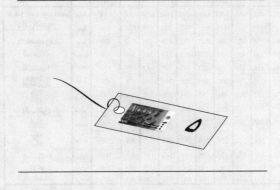
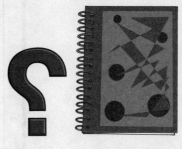

_____

_____

_____

_____

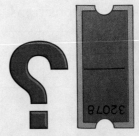

_____

_____

Living Language لغتنا الحيّة

lughatunal-Hayya

المطبوعة	الإصدار	سعر الاشتراك السنوي قبل الخصم ريال	| عدد المطبوعات												
			1	2	3	4	5	6	7	8	9	10	11	12	13
			10%	14%	18%	22%	25%	28%	31%	34%	37%	40%	43%	46%	50%
	يومية	1400	1260	1204	1148	1092	1050	1008	966	924	882	840	798	756	700
	يومية	900	810	774	738	702	675	648	621	594	567	540	513	486	450
	يومية	900	810	774	738	702	675	648	621	594	567	540	513	486	450
المجلة	أسبوعية	630	567	542	517	491	473	454	435	416	397	378	359	340	315
	أسبوعية	630	567	542	517	491	473	454	435	416	397	378	359	340	315
	شهرية	420	378	361	344	328	315	302	290	277	265	252	239	227	210
	١١ عدد في السنة	390	351	335	320	304	293	281	269	257	246	234	222	211	195
السامرين	أسبوعية	300	270	258	246	234	225	216	207	198	189	180	171	162	150
	أسبوعية	300	270	258	246	234	225	216	207	198	189	180	171	162	150
	أسبوعية	320	288	275	262	250	240	230	221	211	202	192	182	173	160
	شهرية	180	162	155	148	140	135	130	124	119	113	108	103	97	90
	أسبوعية	320	288	275	262	250	240	230	221	211	202	192	182	173	160
الجميلة	١١ عدد في السنة	180	162	155	148	140	135	130	124	119	113	108	103	97	90
الإجمالي		6870													3435

جدول حملة الاشتراكات المخفضة لعام ٩٦/١٩٩٧م

R **Look at the clippings to find the information requested below.**

1. A. Circle the two years referred to in the table and write them in English.

    _____

    B. If you buy something in Lebanon and need to give the merchant the currency bill shown in the clipping, how much are you paying?

    _____

2. Circle all the examples of the letters ج , ح , and خ in the clippings and write them below in the four different positions:

Final	Medial	Initial	Independent

Unit 4

الجغرافيا
ajjughraafia
Geography

جبل
jabal

وادي
waadi

نهر
nahr

بحر
baHr

محيط
muHeeT

أرض
arD

مدينة
madeena

قرية
qarya

صحراء
SaHraa'

بحيرة
buHayra

غابة
ghaaba

بلد
balad

ولاية / محافظة
wilaaya / muHaafaDHa

Lebanon (لبنان)
lubnaan

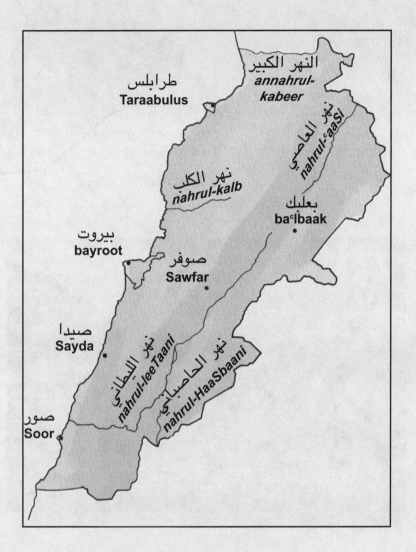

طرابلس
Taraabulus

النهر الكبير
annahrul-kabeer

نهر العاصي
nahrul-aaSi

نهر الكلب
nahrul-kalb

بعلبك
baᶜlbaak

بيروت
bayroot

صوفر
Sawfar

صيدا
Sayda

نهر الليطاني
nahrul-leeTaani

نهر الحاصباني
nahrul-HaaSbaani

صور
Soor

Roman ruins near Beirut's St. George Church

Important Cities

Beirut (بيروت bayroot), the capital of Lebanon, is located on the eastern shores of the Mediterranean Sea. It has a population of about two million people. It is the business, commercial, administrative, and cultural center of the country. Before the civil war, the city was called the "Paris of the Middle East" due to its cosmopolitan nature. It has an important seaport that once served as a hub for the entire Middle East. Downtown Beirut, recently rebuilt after it was ravaged by the civil war, is regaining its status as an exclusive

and elegant service center. The downtown is a combination of renovated old building facades blended with modern, stylish architecture. The city has a number of fancy beach hotels as well as hundreds of prestigious restaurants that serve Lebanese and international foods. Beirut boasts an important museum that houses a large collection of Phoenician artifacts. It also has many art galleries and a dozen universities. Beirut is considered to be the most religiously diverse city in the Middle East, home to five Muslim sects and 12 Christian denominations. In addition, it has a modern sports arena and the largest number of publishing houses in the region.

Theater at Leptis Magna, Libya

Tripoli (طرابلس Taraabulus), the second-largest city in Lebanon, has a population of about 600,000 inhabitants. The city is so ancient that almost every civilization that once inhabited the Middle East left its mark there. It is located on the eastern shores of the Mediterranean Sea about 62 miles north of Beirut. Tripoli is divided into two main districts: *Al-Mina* and old Tripoli. It has the second-largest seaport in Lebanon. Tripoli has 14 major antiquity sites, mainly dating back to the era of the Mamluks and the Crusaders. The city also has Almansuri Mosque, built in 1294 by the Mamluks, which is in fact the oldest mosque in Lebanon. *Qal'at Taraabulus,* one of the oldest Islamic castles in the region, was built in the year 636 A.D. In addition, Tripoli is famous for its orange orchards. The name *fayHaa',* which means "aroma," is used to describe the city. When the orange orchards blossom, the scent fills the city with a sweet smell. Tripoli is also known for its famous desserts, namely *Baqlaawa* and *Halaawa.*

Sidon, Lebanon

Sidon (صيدا Sayda), the third-largest city in Lebanon, is located on the coast about 31 miles south of Beirut. A city with a population of about 200,000, it is also as old as history. Some evidence suggests that the city dates as far back as 6000 B.C. Successive civilizations occupied Sidon, including the Phoenicians, Persians, Greeks, as well as the Romans. Many ancient sites are scattered around Sidon, most of them in total ruins. The Crusaders castle is an important landmark of the city. The temple of *Eshmoun,* the Persian Emperor, is also a site of antiquity that gives Sidon its unique character. Sidon is

nown for its famous sweets, notably the *Sanyoora*. It is also famous for oranges and bananas. Sidon is onsidered the commercial and administrative center for South Lebanon.

olumns at the Thermal Baths, Carthage

Tyre (صور Soor), the fourth-largest city in Lebanon, is located on the coast of the eastern Mediterranean about 51 miles south of Beirut. It is also considered an ancient city that dates back to the third millennium B.C. Successive empires inhabited the city, most famously the Phoenicians, who made it the gateway to the Mediterranean for trade. From Tyre the Phoenicians expanded their domains as far as the Atlantic Ocean. In 815 B.C., they founded Carthage, which ater became the main rival of the Roman Empire. Tyre has a current population of about 140,000. Today he city is famous for its covered markets, or *souks*. Tyre also has great lemon and tangerine orchards.

Baalbeck (بعلبك baʿalbak), a city that was once a jewel in the Roman Empire, has a well-preserved Roman castle, which was built around 300 B.C. It is one of the greatest antiquity sites in the world. The cas-le has the temples of Roman gods: Baccus, Jupiter, Venus, and Mercury. Located at the northern tip of the Baqaaʿ Valley, the most fertile land in the Middle East, the city is 53 miles east of Beirut. Baalbeck is famous or its annual festival that attracts musicians and artists from around the world.

Sofar (صوفر Sawfar), located about 15 miles east of Beirut, is 4,500 feet above the sea. It is onsidered one of the best summer resorts in the Middle East and was the summer resort for both the Ottoman and French rulers. It is situated on a hill overlooking a stretch of mountains and valleys vith clean air and fresh water sources. Although Sawfar has not developed into a commercial resort own, it has however maintained its status as a summer residential area for wealthy Lebanese families.

Important Rivers

Litani (نهر الليطاني nahrul-leeTaani), the largest river in Lebanon, springs out of the northern mountains hat form the border between Lebanon and Syria. It flows south, irrigating almost the entire Baqaaʿ Valley. It urves west a few miles from the southern Lebanese border and heads west into the Mediterranean sea adja-ent to the city of Tyre.

Orontes (نهر العاصي nahral-ᶜaaSi) is known as the rebel river since it springs out of the same area a the Litani but flows north into Syria until it reaches the Mediterranean in Turkey. In Lebanon, the river has a number of famous restaurants on its banks that are filled with tourists during the summertime.

Hasbani (الحاصباني HaaSbaani) is a small river that springs out of the Wazzani source at the bottome of Mount Hermon and flows south to meet the *Banias* river. A few miles further, it becomes the famous Jordan river. John the Baptist used the water of this river to baptize Jesus.

Annahr al-kabeer (النهر الكبير annahrul-kabeer) forms the northern border between Lebanon and Syria. It flows West into the Mediterranean Sea. This river is mentioned in the Bible. A number of Phoenician antiquities were found on the banks of this river.

Nahr al-Kalb (نهر الكلب nahrul-kalb) springs out of the *Jaᶜeeta* Grotto in North Lebanon and flows 16 miles west into the Medterranean. Al-Kalb River is also a historic river that once served as the buffer between the northern and the southern civilizations. It was on the banks of this river that a cuneiform with the Phoenician alphabet was discovered, which benefited scholars worldwide who study ancient languages.

A view towards the mountains in the direction of Aagoura, Lebanon

Tabbouleh is a salad of Lebanese origin consisting chiefly of cracked wheat, tomatoes, parsley, mint, onions, lemon juice, and olive oil.

Important Facts

- Lebanon has the most religously diverse population in the Middle East.
- Many Lebanese speak French and / or English, in addition to Arabic.
- Lebanon has a democratic system with political representation on the basis of religion instead of political parties.
- Lebanon went through a brutal civil war that lasted from 1975 to 1990.
- Lebanon is the second-richest country in water resources in the Middle East, after Iraq.
- The first alphabet was invented in Lebanon.

- Lebanon is famous for *Kibbi* and *Tabbouli*.

- Lebanon is about the size of New Hampshire.

- Lebanon was founded in the 16th century by Fakhr Edwin, a Druze Emir.

- Lebanon's topography consists mainly of mountains and valleys.

- There are no deserts in Lebanon.

his tablet is inscribed using the Phoenician al- habet, which became the prototype for other lphabets.

In this aerial view of central Lebanon, the Litani Dam is in the foreground and the labal al-barook Mountains are in the background.

The statue on Martyr Square in Beirut is full of bullet holes from the civil war.

Iraq (العراق)

al ʿiraac

Important Cities

Baghdad (بغداد baghdaad), the capital and largest city of Iraq, is located in the central part of the country on the Tigris River. The city has a population of about seven million scattered on both banks of the river and connected by 11 bridges. It is the administrative, commercial, and cultural center of Iraq. Initially built as a circular walled-in city, it dates back to 1800 B.C. However, it was not until the 8th century A.D., under the Islamic dynasty of the Abbasids, that it reached its zenith as the intellectual and cultural birthplace of Islamic civilization. It was a place where scholars came to share ideas and writings on philosophy, math, astronomy, and medicine. Baghdad had the first university, *Dar- ul Hikma* (830 A.D.). Trade and commerce flourished during this time and continued for the next three centuries. Still, the greatness of Baghdad lasted only until 1258 when the Mongol hordes came from the east and ransacked the city to its foundations. The Mongols burned all the intellectual centers and killed most of the inhabitants of the city. In the following centuries, Baghdad experienced a cultural and economic decline as various groups occupied it. Yet Baghdad became prosperous again as the oil boom of the 1970's generated a lot of income. The city of Baghdad was rebuilt with a modern high way system and the latest in water and electrical technologies. Museums and art flourished. Much of the city was once again destroyed when the United States bombed it before invading in 2003.

Basra, (البصرة albaSra), the second-largest city in Iraq after Baghdad, has a population of about one million people. Located near the Persian Gulf, it is known for rich agricultural products like rice, wheat, and dates. It is a city with many canals, allowing residents to get around using boats much of the time. Some have called it the "Venice of the Middle East." The people of this area come from diverse religious backgrounds. There are *sheeʿa* Muslims, Sunni Muslims, and even a small number of Christians living and working together. This city is important for political reasons due to the high number of oil wells in the area. It has an oil refinery with an estimated capacity of 140,000 barrels of oil per day.

Najaf (النجف, annajaf), located to the south of the capital city Baghdad on the Euphrates River, has a population of about 600,000. It is a holy city for the *sheeʿa* sect of Islam since the shrine of Imam Ali is located there. Annajaf is the city where *sheeʿa* pilgrims visit the shrine of the Imam Ali Mosque. The city is the religious and political center for the *sheeʿa* of Iraq. The *Hindiyya* canal, built in 1803, doubled the population of the city from 30,000 to 60,000.

The Christian crosses of a Beirut cathedral surround a minaret of al Amin mosque.

Mosul (الموصل, almooSul), which lies 250 miles to the north of Baghdad, has a population of over a million people. This city is known for making a cotton fabric called muslin, which was introduced to Europe in the 17th century and had many uses, for example, as stage backdrops in the theater. It is also known for manufacturing and exporting quality marble. The city sits on both banks of the Tigris River, which can be crossed by five bridges. Mosul boasts the highest concentration of Christians in all of Iraq. There are many churches and monasteries which date back to the second century A.D. Traditionally, Mosul was a city of great ethnic diversity including Arabs, Kurds, Armenians, Muslims, and Christians. The University of Mosul is one of the largest and most prestigious colleges in the Middle East.

Workers at a Kirkuk oil drilling facility

Kirkuk (كركوك, karkook), located about 150 miles north of the capital city of Baghdad, has a population of about 700,000. It is best known for having the largest oil sites in Iraq. Kirkuk has been pumping large amounts of oil for the past 70 years, providing more than 50% of Iraq's oil. Its population encompasses a diverse population, including Kurds, Arabs, Turks, and Assyrians. However, there is a Kurdish majority and they dominate the government

institutions. The *al-Qaysariyyah* Market is the oldest market, or *souk,* in Kirkuk. It was built in 1855 during Ottoman rule. The layout of the market is said to symbolize the passage of time on earth. It consists of 365 stores, which represent the days in a year; 12 rooms on the second floor, which represent the 12 months of the year; and 24 aisles which represent the hours in a day. Finally, there are seven doors that represent the days of the week.

Karbala, Iraq

Karbala (كربلاء, karbalaa') is located about 60 miles southwest of Baghdad. The city was built around the shrine of Imam alHusayn, the son of Imam Ali, and the grandson of Prophet Mohammad, who was martyred with his brother and his companions in 680 A.D. Karbala is considered a holy city for the *shee'a* sect of Islam. *Shee'a* pilgrims travel to Karbala to pay homage to the shrine of Imam alHusayn. The city has grown over the years around the shrines, with a population today of nearly 600,000. It has more than two dozen Islamic *madrasa,* or universities, and more than a hundred *masjid.*

Important Rivers

The important river Tigris (دجلة dijla) rises out of the Anatolian Hills and Lake Hazar in Turkey, and enters Iraq in the North. Many tributaries feed into it, including the *Zab*. It passes through major Iraqi cities, including Mosul and Baghdad, flowing south where it meets the Euphrates north of Basra to form *shattal-'arab*. The Tigris pours into the Persian Gulf.

Tigris River, Iraq

The Euphrates (الفرات **alfuraat**) rises out of Mount Ararat in Armenia and Anatonlia in Turkey, and has many small tributaries that feed into it in Turkey before it enters Syria and Iraq. In Iraq the river passes through the city of Karbala and Najaf and flows south until it meets the Tigris to form *shattal-arab*. It pours into the Persian Gulf after it passes the city of Basra. Historically, the land between the Tigris and Euphrates witnessed a number of flourishing civilizations. It is known as the "land between the two rivers," or Mesopotamia.

The Euphrates River near Khan EL Baghdadi, Iraq

Important Facts

- The first law, called *sharee'at Hamurabi*, was discovered in Iraq.
- Iraq boasts the greatest water resources in the Middle East.
- Iraq has the second-largest oil reserves in the world, after Saudi Arabia.
- Iraqis are considered to be among the best educated people in the Arab world.
- Iraq has the most art institutions and artists in the Arab world.
- Iraq has the second-largest *Shee'a* sect, after Iran.

A Match each Arabic word with its English equivalent.

A. desert
B. mountain
C. village
D. river
E. city
F. sea
G. state
H. country
I. forest
J. valley
K. ocean
L. earth

1. ـــــــــ ولاية wilaaya
2. ـــــــــ صحراء 'SaHraa
3. ـــــــــ جبل jabal
4. ـــــــــ محيط muHeeT
5. ـــــــــ غابة ghaaba
6. ـــــــــ بحر baHr
7. ـــــــــ وادي waadi
8. ـــــــــ أرض 'arD
9. ـــــــــ مدينة madeena
10. ـــــــــ بلد balad
11. ـــــــــ نهر nahr
12. ـــــــــ قرية qarya

B Write the letter of each city on the map next to its name below.

لبنان (lubnaan)

1. ـــــــــ بعلبك (ba'albak)
2. ـــــــــ صيدا (Sayda)
3. ـــــــــ طرابلس (Tarabulus)
4. ـــــــــ صوفر (Sawfar)
5. ـــــــــ صور (Soor)
6. ـــــــــ بيروت (bayroot)

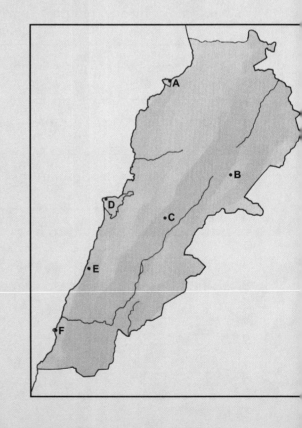

العراق (al'iraaq)

7. ـــــــ النجف (annajaf)

8. ـــــــ بغداد (baghdaad)

9. ـــــــ كركوك (kirkook)

10. ـــــــ الموصل (almooSul)

11. ـــــــ البصرة (albaSra)

12. ـــــــ كربلاء (karbalaa')

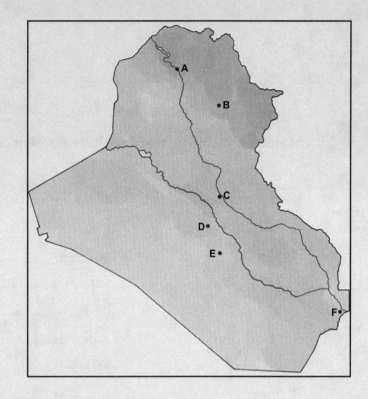

C **Identify the cities described below.**

1. has 14 antiquity sites

_____

2. provides the most oil

_____

3. has famous Roman temples

_____

4. is connected by 11 bridges

_____

5. is known for its great summer weather

_____

6. has 12 Christian denominations and five Muslim sects

_____

7. is the second-largest city in Iraq

_____

8. is known for a famous desert called *sanyoora*

_____

9. has the shrine if Imam Ali

_____

10. is a river that flows north and pours into the Mediterranean

_____

D Identify the geographical features described below.

1. the longest river in Lebanon

   _____

2. has two major rivers merge within its vicinity

   _____

3. the sea located west of Lebanon

   _____

4. the name of the body of water that borders Iraq and Kuwait

   _____

5. the name of the mountains bordering Lebanon in the East

   _____

E Match Column *A* with Column *B*.

B	A
A. becomes the Jordan River	1. _____ بغداد baghdaad
B. a city known for muslin and marble	2. _____ نهر الحاصباني nahrul-HaaSbaani
C. first written law bears his name	3. _____ النجف annajaf
D. capital of the Abbasid Dynasty	4. _____ بيروت bayroot
E. a city with a newly-built downtown	5. _____ نهر الكلب Nahrul-kalb
F. a city used by the Phoenicians for their trade expansion	6. _____ حمورابي Hamooraabi
G. a city known as the "Venice of the Middle East"	7. _____ الموصل almooSul
H. a city with a market that has 365 stores, which recalls the days of the year	8. _____ صور Soor
I. where an inscription of the first known alphabet was found	9. _____ البصرة albaSra
J. located on the Euphrates River	10. _____ كركوك kirkook
K. the area where the Tigris and Euphrates meet	11. _____ شط العرب shaTTul-ᶜarab

F **Name the city associated with each illustration.**

.1

_____

.2

_____

.3

_____

.4

_____

.5

_____

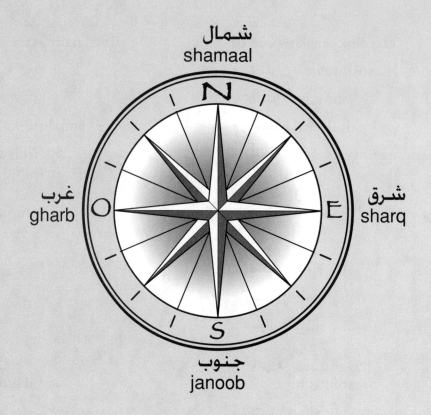

شمال
shamaal

غرب
gharb

شرق
sharq

جنوب
janoob

G Circle the letter representing the word that best completes the phrase.

3. الموصل تقع في ـــــ العراق
almooSul taqaʿ fee... alʿiraaq

أ. جنوب janoob

ب. شرق sharq

ج. شمال shamaal

د. غرب gharb

4. صوفر تقع في ـــــ لبنان
Sawfar taqaʿ fee... lubnaan

أ. بحيرات buHayraat

ب. مدن mudun

ج. جبال jibaal

د. قرى qura

1. بعلبك هي ـــــ
baʿalbak hiya....

أ. نهر nahr

ب. جبل jabal

ج. بلد balad

د. مدينة madeena

2. طرابلس مدينة على ـــــ
Tarabulus madeena ʿala....

أ. البحر الأبيض المتوسط
albahrul- 'abiaDul-mutawassit

ب. الخليج العربي alkhaleejul-ʿarabi

ج. نهر الليطاني nahrul-leeTaani

د. نهر الفرات nahrul-furaat

5. أطول نهر يمر في العراق هو ـــــ
aTwal nahr yamur fil-ʿiraaq huwa....

أ. الفرات alfuraat

ب. دجلة dijla

ج. النهر الكبير annahrul-kabeer

د. نهر العاصي nahrul-ʿaaSi

8. بعلبك مشهورة بـ
baʿalbak mashhoora be

أ. الشوارع ashshwaariʿ

ب. المدن almudun

ج. المحيط almuHeeT

د. القلعة الرومانية alqalʿar- roomaaniyya

6. لبنان ليس فيه ـــــ
lubnaan laysa feehi....

أ. وادي waadi

ب. أرض 'arD

ج. غابة ghaaba

د. صحراء 'SaHraa

9. لا يحد العراق أو لبنان
laa yaHudul-ʿiraaq 'aw lubnaan

أ. بحر baHr

ب. محيط muHeeT

ج. خليج khaleej

د. جبال jibaal

7. يحد العراق ـــــ دول
yaHudul-ʿiraaq... duwal

أ. أربع 'arbaʿ

ب. خمس khams

ج. ست sitt

د. سبع sabaʿ

10. طرابلس هي ـــــ صور
Taraabulus hiya... Soor

أ. شرق sharq

ب. جنوب janoob

ج. غرب gharb

د. شمال shamaal

H **Imagine that you are a tour guide hired to lead a group of scholars from the United States on a cultural and historical tour of Iraq. Name three cities you would show them and tell what they would see there.**

_____

_____

_____

_____

_____

_____

_____

_____

_____

_____

I Name three places you would like to visit if you were the winner of a three-week vacation to Lebanon. (You get to choose the season.) Tell why you selected these places. What would you see or do there?

_____

_____

_____

_____

_____

_____

_____

_____

_____

_____

_____

_____

J دورك! (*dawrak!*) Travel Agency Role-play! Pretend that you are going on a trip to an Arabic-speaking country. Ask for recommendations of places to visit. Your friend will play the part of the travel agent and make several suggestions. Include saying "hello" and "thank you" in Arabic!

How Do I Write the Arabic Alphabet?

khaa خ and *daal* د in the four different positions

Final	Medial	Initial	Independent
خ	ـخـ	خـ	خ
بطيخ	يخت	خوخ	جوخ
Writing Practice			

ـد	ـد	د	د
عيد	بدر	دور	زاد
Writing Practice			

Symtalk

K In the space, write the correct word or expression in Arabic.

L Say the sentences, then write them in Arabic.

_____

_____

_____

.4

_____

.5

_____

Work with a partner. Ask the question or give the answer. Then, write the dialogue.

.1

_____ _____

.2

_____ _____

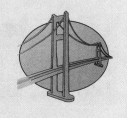

.3

_____ _____

_____ _____ .

_____ _____ .

Proverb

نيّال من له مرقد عنزة
في جبل لبنان.
**niyyaal mann lahu marqad
ᶜanza fee jabal lubnaan.**
Lucky is the one who has a goat's
shelter in Mount Lebanon.

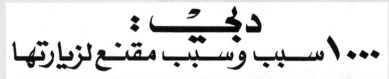

دبــيّ :
١٠٠٠ ســبب وسـتّب مقنع لزيارتها

من الداخل

التمتع بجمال لبنان لا يكتمل
الا بزيارة اجمل موقع طبيعي

N **Look at the clippings to find the information requested below.**

1. Find the word for "Dubai," circle it, and then write it.

_____

2. Circle all the examples of the letter د and any other two other letters that you recognize in the clippings and write them below in the four different positions:

Final	Medial	Initial	Independent

Unit 5

البيت
'albayt
House

English	Transliteration	Arabic
Where do you live?	'ayna taskun?	أليشا (f.): أين تسكن؟
I live in a house in Beirut.	'askun fi bayt fi beirut.	هشام (m.): أسكن في بيت في بيروت.
Where is the garden?	'ayanal-muntazah?	سميرة (f.): أين المنتزه؟
The garden is over there.	almuntazah hunaak.	أنيس (m.): المنتزه هناك.
Where's the parking garage?	'aynaal-mawqaf / alkaaraaj?	طلال (m.): أين الموقف / الكاراج؟
It's behind the garden.	waraa'al-muntazah.	أميرة (m.): وراء المنتزه.
How many bedrooms are there in your house?	kam ghurfat nawm fee baytuki?	أديبة (f.): كم غرفة نوم في بيتك؟
There are four bedrooms in my house.	hunaka 'arbaᶜ ghuraf nawm fee bayti.	منية (f.): هناك أربع غرف نوم في بيتي.

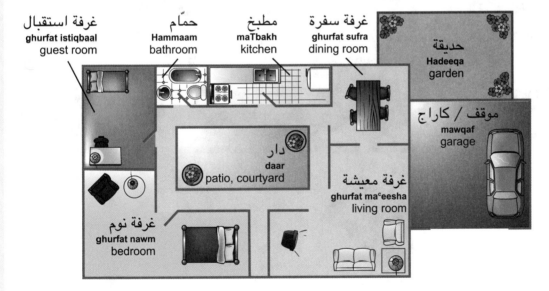

غرفة استقبال
ghurfat istiqbaal
guest room

حمّام
Hammaam
bathroom

مطبخ
maTbakh
kitchen

غرفة سفرة
ghurfat sufra
dining room

حديقة
Hadeeqa
garden

موقف / كاراج
mawqaf
garage

دار
daar
patio, courtyard

غرفة معيشة
ghurfat maᶜeesha
living room

غرفة نوم
ghurfat nawm
bedroom

- The article "the" (ال) is a prefix applied to both feminine and masculine nouns. It changes indefinite nouns to definite nouns.
- The word منتزه (muntazah) can be replaced by the word حديقة (Hadeeqa).
- Another word for bedroom is أوضة نوم ('awDat nawm).
- Hospitality is a very important part of Arab culture. Being gracious to one's guests includes making them feel at home.

قصر
QaSr

شقة
shiqqa

بيت خاص
bayt khaaS

شاليه
shaaleh

بناية شقق
binayat shuqaq

خيمة
khayma

شقة *(shiqqa)* refers to a condominium or apartment.

A Write the Arabic word for each numbered room.

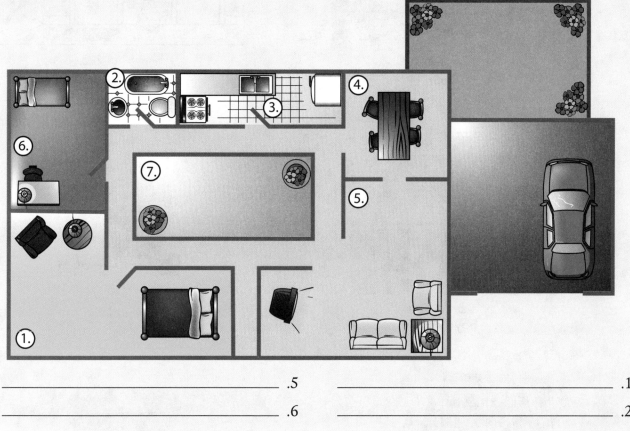

_____ .5	_____ .1
_____ .6	_____ .2
_____ .7	_____ .3
	_____ .4

B Complete the sentences in Arabic.

1. في (cook) أطبخ ._____
   'aTbukh fee....

2. في (sleep) أنام ._____
   'anaam fee....

3. في (eat) آكل ._____
   aakul fee....

4. في (take a bath) أستحم ._____
   'astaHim fee....

5. ‏ألعب (play) في _____ .
'al‘ab fee....

6. ‏أرتاح (relax) في _____ .
'artaaH fee....

C Circle the English equivalent of the Arabic word.

dining room	kitchen	bedroom	‏غرفة السفرة ghurfatus-sufra
bedroom	kitchen	bathroom	‏المطبخ almaTbakh
living room	bathroom	bedroom	‏غرفة النوم ghurfatun-nawm
bathroom	kitchen	dining room	‏الحمّام alHammaam
dining room	bathroom	living room	‏غرفة المعيشة ghurfatul-ma‘eesha

D In which room would you find the following items? In Arabic, please.

1. dining table _____

2. refrigerator _____

3. alarm clock _____

4. piano _____

5. shower _____

6. stove _____

7. sofa _____

8. tablecloth _____

9. toilet _____

10. dresser _____

E Identify each location with the appropriate Arabic word.

1. place to sleep when camping _____

2. renter's residence in a building _____

3. homeowner's residence _____

4. millionaire's residence _____

5. place to park a car at home _____

Read the paragraph. Then, choose the correct words to complete each sentence in Arabic.

بيتي جميل. أسكن مع أسرتي. أحب بيتي. هناك ثلاث غرف نوم
bayti jameel. 'askun ma⁶ 'usrati. 'uHibbu bayti. hunaaka thalaath ghuraf nawm
وكاراج. هناك زهور كثيرة في الحديقة ونافورة في الدار.
wakaaraaj. hunaaka zuhoor katheera fil-Hadeeqa wanaafoora fid-daar.

١. بيتي ــ.
bayti....

٢. أسكن مع أسرتي ــــــــــــــــــــــــــــــــ.
'askun ma⁶ 'usrati....

٣. ــــــــــــــــــــــــــــــــ بيتي.
...bayti.

٤. هناك ثلاث غرف نوم و ــــــــــــــــــــــــــ.
hunaka thalaath ghuraf nawm wa....

٥. هناك ـــــــــــــــــــــــ كثيرة في الحديقة ــــــــــــــــــــــــ في الدار.
hunaka... katheera fil Hadeeqa...   fid daar.

البيت

الأسرة

I live	أسكن	with	مع	pretty	جميل
	'askun		ma⁶		jameel
flowers	زهور	I like	أحب	here	هنا
	zuhoor		'auHibb		huna
fountain	نافورة ماء				
	nafoorat maa'				

G لنتكلّم! (*linatakallam!*) Point to a picture of a room in a house. Ask your speaking partner in Arabic: هل هذه غرفة نوم؟ (*hal haadhihi ghurfat nawm?*) He / she should answer: لا ، هذا مطبخ (*laa, haadha maTbakh*) or نعم هذه غرفة نوم (*na'am, haadhihi ghurfat nawm*). Take turns asking and answering questions about all the rooms in the house.

H لنتكلّم! (*linatakallam!*) Point to one of the types of residences shown in your book. As you do this, ask your classmate where an imaginary student lives. He / she should answer appropriately.

مثال:

mithaal:

Example:

يسكن في شقة.   (*points to an apartment*) أين يسكن قيصر؟

yaskun fee shuqqa.   'ayna yaskun qaySar?

He lives in an apartment.   *Where does Caesar live?*

Proverb

" من يسكن في بيت من زجاج لا يرمي الناس بالحجارة.

mann yaskun fee bayt min zujaaj la yarmin-naas bilHijaara.

The one who lives in a glass house shouldn't throw rocks at people. **"**

How Do I Write the Arabic Alphabet?

raa ر and *zaa* ز in the four different positions

Final	Medial	Initial	Independent
ـر	ـر	ر	ر
حبر	فرس	رأس	فأر
Writing Practice			
ـر	ـر	ر	ر
حبر	فرس	رأس	فأر

Final	Medial	Initial	Independent
ـز	ـز	ز	ز
لوز	جزر	زيت	خرز
Writing Practice			
ـز	ـز	ز	ز
لوز	جزر	زيت	خرز

Symtalk

I In Arabic, write the word or expression that corresponds to each picture.

J Say the sentences, then write them in Arabic.

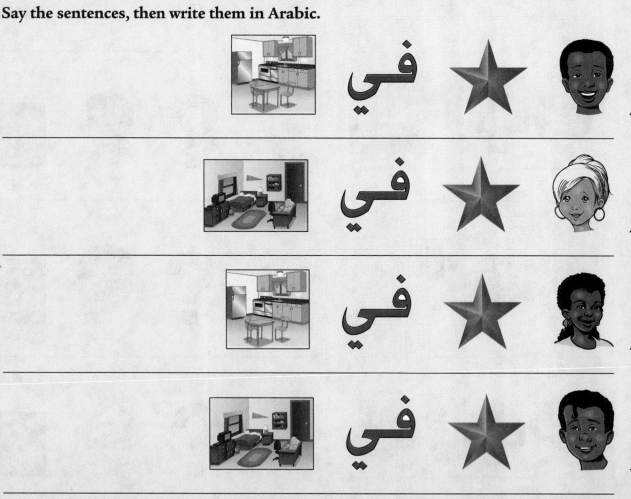

K Work with a partner. Ask the question or give the answer. Then write the dialogue.

.1
_____
_____

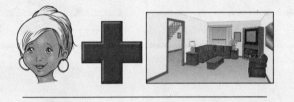   
.2
_____
_____

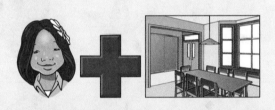
.3
_____
_____

.4
_____
_____

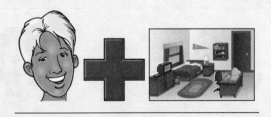
.5
_____
_____

L **Look at the clipping to find the information requested below.**

1. A. How many times is the word for "Lebanon" mentioned? Write the number in Arabic.

   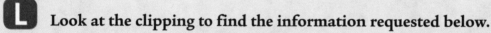

   B. Circle two listed telephone numbers and copy one in the blank using Indian numbers.

   _____

2. Circle all the examples of the letter ر and any other two letters that you recognize in the clipping and write them below in the four different positions:

Final	Medial	Initial	Independent

Unit 6

العائلة

al^caa'ila

Family

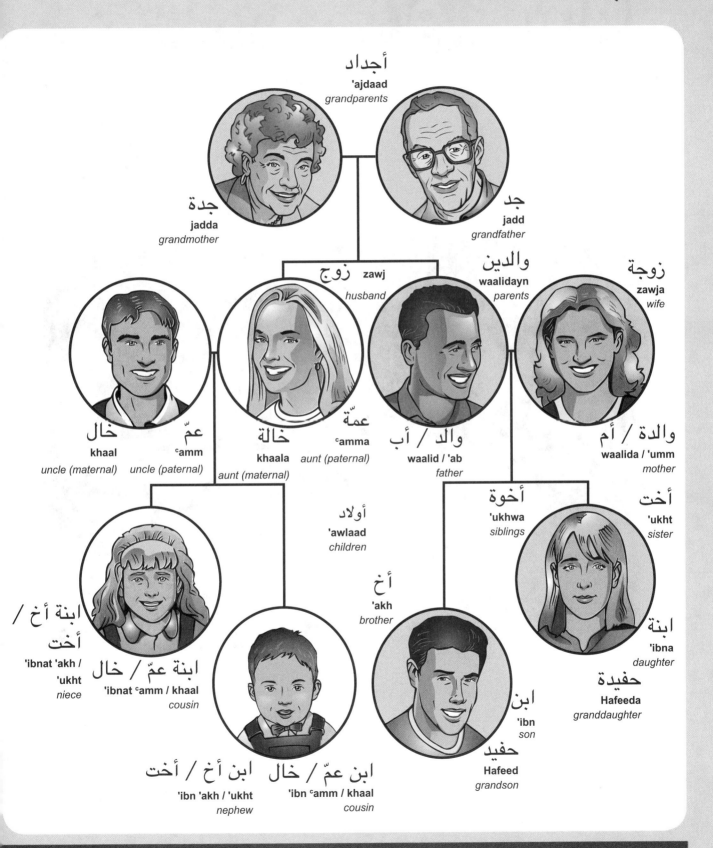

أجداد
'ajdaad
grandparents

جدة
jadda
grandmother

جد
jadd
grandfather

زوج
zawj
husband

والدين
waalidayn
parents

زوجة
zawja
wife

خال
khaal
uncle (maternal)

عمّ
ᶜamm
uncle (paternal)

خالة
khaala
aunt (maternal)

عمّة
ᶜamma
aunt (paternal)

والد / أب
waalid / 'ab
father

والدة / أم
waalida / 'umm
mother

أخت
'ukht
sister

أولاد
'awlaad
children

أخوة
'ukhwa
siblings

أخ
'akh
brother

ابنة أخ / أخت
'ibnat 'akh / 'ukht
niece

ابنة عمّ / خال
'ibnat ᶜamm / khaal
cousin

ابنة
'ibna
daughter

حفيدة
Hafeeda
granddaughter

ابن
'ibn
son

حفيد
Hafeed
grandson

ابن عمّ / خال
'ibn ᶜamm / khaal
cousin

ابن أخ / أخت
'ibn 'akh / 'ukht
nephew

من هوَ؟
mann huwa?
Who is this?

هو أخي.
huwa 'akhi.
He is my brother.

هل هما والداكِ؟
hal huma walidaaki?
Are they your parents?

نعم، والدتي اسمها سامية ووالدي اسمه سليم.
naᶜam, waalidati 'ismuha saamia wawaalidi 'ismuhu saleem.
Yes, my mother's name is Samia and my father's name is Saleem.

من الأولاد؟
manal-awlad?
Who are the children?

هما حفيدي وحفيدتي.
huma Hafeedi wa Hafeedati.
They're my granddaughter and my grandson.

هل سمير وليلى وباسم أخوة؟
hal sameer wa layla wa baasim 'ukhwa?
Are Sameer and Samia and Baasim siblings?

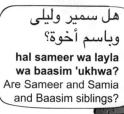

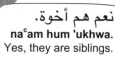

نعم هم أخوة.
naᶜam hum 'ukhwa.
Yes, they are siblings.

Don't forget! **laa tansa**	لاتنسى
alijtimaᶜul ᶜaa'ili *Family Reunion*	الاجتماع العائلي
Guests **Duyoof**	ضيوف
alᶜamma jameela wa zawjuha *Aunt Jameela and her husband*	العمّة جميلة وزوجها
'ukhti wa 'awlaaduha *my sister and her children*	أختي وأولادها
alkhaala yaaqoot wabanaatuha *Aunt Yaqoot and her daughters*	الخالة ياقوت وبناتها
alᶜamm jurj wazawjatuhu *Uncle George and his wife*	العمّ جورج وزوجته
nadia waTifluha *Nadia and her baby*	ناديا و طفلها
alkhaal faaris wa'usratuhu *Uncle Faris and his family*	الخال فارس وأسرته

❀❀❀❀❀

سعيد (.m): أين أقاربك؟
saᶜeed: 'ayna 'aqaribuka?
Where are your relatives?

مجيد (.m): جدي وجدتي في الداخل وأعمامي و عمّاتي في الحديقة.
majeed: jaddi wa jaddati fid-daakhil wa'aᶜmaami waᶜammaati fil-Hadeeqa.
My grandparents are inside and my uncles and aunts are in the garden.

طفل
Tifl
child (m.)

ولد
walad
boy

طفلة
Tifla
child (f.)

رجل
rajul
man

بنت
bint
girl

امرأة
'imra'a
woman

رضيع
raDeeᶜ
baby

Note: Nouns that end with ة (*taa' marbooTa*) are feminine nouns, for example:

أديبة (*f.*)   أديب (*m.*)
'adeeba   'adeeb

A Indicate Maya's, Basem's, and Ghazi's relationship to each family member listed.

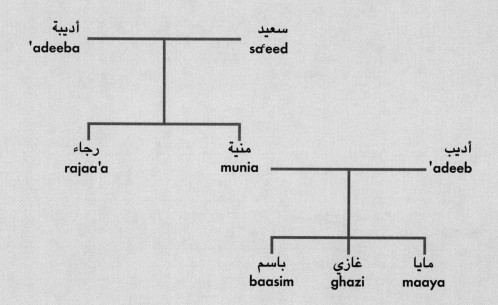

مايا هي....
maaya hiya...

غازي. _____ .1
...ghaazi.

منية. _____ .2
...munia.

سعيد. _____ .3
...saʿeed.

باسم. _____ .4
...baasim.

أديبة. _____ .5
...'adeeba.

6. _____ رجاء.
   ...rajaa'.

7. _____ أديب.
   ...'adeeb.

منية هي....
munia hiya....

8. _____ مايا وغازي وباسم.
   ...maaya waghaazi wabaasim.

9. _____ أديب.
   ...'adeeb.

10. _____ رجاء.
    ...rajaa'.

11. _____ سعيد وأديبة.
    ...saᶜeed wa'adeeba.

سعيد هو....
saᶜeed huwa....

12. _____ مايا وغازي وباسم.
    ...maaya waghaazi wabaasim.

13. _____ منية ورجاء.
    ...munia warajaa'.

14. _____ أديبة.
    ...'adeeba.

B **Who is this? Write in Arabic, please.**

> مثال:
> mithaal:
> *Example:*
>
> ابنة والدي ووالدتي هي أختي.
> 'ibnat waalidy wawaalidaty hiya 'ukhti.
> *The daughter of my father and my mother is my sister.*

1. أخت والدتي هي _____.
   'ukht waalidaty hiya....

2. أخت والدي هي _____.
   'ukht waalidi hiya....

3. أخو والدي هو _____
   waalid waalidi huwa....

٣. أخو والدتي هو _____.
'akhoo waalidaty huwa....

٤. والدة والدتي هي _____.
waalidat waalidaty hiya....

٥. والد والدي هو _____.
waalid waalidi huwa....

C **Who am I? Fill in the blank with the correct word in Arabic.**

1. I am your father's son. I am _____.

2. I am your niece's mother. I am _____.

3. I am your brother's son. I am _____.

4. I am your mother's mother. I am _____.

D **Choose the correct answer.**

3. أين الجدان؟ 'aynal-jaddaan?
   A. on the bench
   B. in the crib
   C. in the foreground

1. أين الوالدان؟ 'aynal-waalidaan?
   A. on the bench
   B. in the crib
   C. in the foreground

2. أين الرضيع؟ 'aynal-raDeeʿ?
   A. on the bench
   B. in the crib
   C. in the foreground

E **What do these questions mean in English?**

١. مَن أنت؟   mann'ant?

_____

٢. مَن أنا؟   mann'anaa?

_____

٣. مَن المرأة؟   manal-mar'a?

_____

F **Complete in Arabic the answers to the following questions. Use the cues in parentheses.**

١. مَن الولد؟   manal-walad? *(son)*

_____ هو
huwa....

٢. مَن البنت؟   manal-bint? *(daughter)*

_____ هي
hiya....

٣. مَن الرجل؟   manar-rajul? *(uncle)*

_____ هو
huwa....

G Read the paragraph and then write it in English. Try to figure out words you don't know from the context.

عائلتي ليست كبيرة. والدي عمره سبعة وثلاثين سنة. والدتي عمرها واحد وثلاثين سنة.
ʿaaʾilati laysat kabeera. waalidi ʿumruhu sabʿa wathalaatheen sana. waalidaty ʿumruha waHid wathalaatheen sana.

أختي اسمها سميرة (.f) وعمرها تسع سنوات. أخي اسمه عماد (.m) وعمره ست سنوات.
ʾukhti ʾismuha sameera wa ʿumruha tisʿ sanawaat. ʾakhi ʾismuhu ʾimaad wa ʿumruhu sitt sanawaat.

اسمي أميرة (.f) وعمري ثلاثة عشر سنة. عائلتي تسكن في جبل لبنان. عندنا بيت واحد فقط.
ʾismi ʾameera waʿumri thalaathata ʿashar sana. ʿaaʾilaati taskun fee jabal lubnaan. ʿindana bayt waHid faqaT.

جدي وجدتي وعمّي يسكنون في مدينة بيروت. عندهم شقة في المدينة.
jaddi wajaddati waʿammy yaskunaan fee madeenat bayroot. ʿindahum shiqqa fil-madeena.

we have	lanaa	لنا	he / she is	huwa / hiya	هوَ / هيَ
they have	lahum	لهم	I am	'anaa	أنا

_____

_____

_____

_____

_____

H لنتكلم! (*linatakallam!*) Ask your speaking partner about five members of his / her family, for example, the person's name and age. Your partner should answer each question. Then, he / she will ask you about your family and you will answer.

مثال:
mithaal:
Example:

A: هل لك أخت؟ hal lak 'ukht? *(Do you have a sister?)*

B: نعم لي أخت. naʿam lee 'ukht. *(Yes, I have a sister.)*

A: ما اسمها؟ maasmuha? *(What is her name?)*

B: اسمها (.f) سميرة. 'ismuha sameera. *(Her name is Sameera.)*

A: ما عمرها؟ maa ʿumruha? *(How old is she?)*

B: عمرها تسع سنوات. ʿumruhaa tisʿ sanawaat. *(She's nine years old.)*

I دورك! (*dawrak!*) Find some family photographs and exchange them with a friend. Holding up your friend's photo first, ask him / her who is in the picture. He / she will identify each person with the correct relationship. Then, reverse roles.

مثال:
mithaal:
Example:

A: من هي/ هو؟
(*Who is she / he?*) mann hiya? / ...huwa?

B: هي جدتي./ هو جدي.
(*She's my grandmother. / He's my grandfather.*) hiya jaddati. / huwa jaddi.

Proverb

"الأقربون أولى بالمعروف.
al'aqraboon awla bilma'roof.
Charity should first be given
to loved ones."

How Do I Write the Arabic Alphabet?

seen س and *sheen* ش in the four different positions

Final	Medial	Initial	Independent
س	ـسـ	سـ	س
كيس	جسر	سيف	رأس
Writing Practice			
ـس	ـسـ	سـ	س
كيس	جسر	سيف	رأس

Final	Medial	Initial	Independent
ش	ـشـ	شـ	ش
ريش	قشر	شيخ	حرش
Writing Practice			
ـش	ـشـ	شـ	ش
ريش	قشر	شيخ	حرش

Symtalk

J In Arabic, write the word or expression that corresponds to each picture.

_____ .6 | _____ .5 | _____ .4 | _____ .3 | _____ .2 | _____ .1

K Say the sentences, then write them in Arabic.

.1   🌟   في

_____

.2   🌟   في

_____

.3   🌟   في

_____

.4   🌟   في

_____

 في ★

L Work with a partner. Ask the question or give the answer. Then, write the dialogue.

  في .1

_____

_____

  في .2

_____

_____

   في .3

_____

_____

  في .4

_____

_____

  في .5

_____

Living Language لغتنا الحيّة

lughatunal-Hayya

M **Look at the clipping to find the information requested below.**

1. A. How many Arabic names are there in this wedding announcement?

   _____

   B. Write one of the names in Arabic.

   _____

2. Circle all the examples of the letters ز , ذ , and س in the clipping and write them below in the four different positions:

Final	Medial	Initial	Independent

Unit 7

الحيوانات

alHayawaanaat

Animals

بقرة
baqara
cow

حمار
Himaar
donkey

عصفور
ªaSfoor
bird

بطة
baTTa
duck

خروف
kharoof
sheep

ديك
deek
rooster

دجاجة
dajaaja
hen

هرّة
hirra
cat

حصان
HiSaan
horse

كلب
kalb
dog

أديبة (.f): تعال يا سلمان! أنا أطعم الحيوانات الآن. أعطي الحصان تفاحة.

'adeeba: taªal ya salmaan. 'ana 'aTªamul-Hayawaanaat al'aan. 'aªTil-HiSaan tuffaHa.

Adeeba: Come on! I'm feeding the animals now. I'm giving the horse an apple.

سلمان (.m): عظيم! أريد مساعدتكِ. هل من الممكن؟

salmaan: ªaDHeem 'ureedu musaaªadatuki, hal minal-mumkin?

Salman: Great! I want to help you. Can I?

أديبة: طبعا يمكنكَ مساعدتي يا سلمان! خذ هذا الدلو من فضلك!

'adeeba: Tabªan yumkinuka musaaªadati yaa salmaan!
khudh haadhad-daloo min faDlak!

Adeeba: Of course you can, Salman! Take this bucket, please!

سلمان: ما اسم الهرّ؟

salmaan: ma-smul hirr?

Salman: What's the cat's name?

أديبة: هذا عنتر.

'adeeba: haadha ªantar.

Adeeba: This is Antar.

سلمان: هل هناكَ دجاج أيضاً؟

salmaan: hal hunaaka dajaaj 'ayDan?

Salman: Are there hens too?

أديبة: نعم، هم وراء الزريبة. جمع البيض من فضلك!

'adeeba: naªam hum waraa'az-zareeba. jammiª albayD min faDlak!

Adeeba: Yes, they're behind the barn. Gather the eggs, please!

في البرية
fil-barriyya
in the country

في الهواء
fil-hawaa'
in the air

بيغاء
babbaghaa'
parrot

في الحقل
fil-Haql
in the field

في الزريبة
fiz-zareeba
in the barn

حيوان
Hayawaan
animal

معزة
ma°za
goat

أرنب
'arnab
rabbit

في الإسطبل
fil-'isTabl
in the stable

في البركة
fil-birka
in the pond

كبيرة
kabeera
big

صغير
Sagheer
little

بيض
bayD
eggs

علي (.m) : ماذا تفعل؟
°ali: maadha taf°al?
Ali: What are you doing?

موسى (.m) : أنا أجمّع البيض.
moosa: 'anaa 'ujammi°l-bayD.
Moosa: I'm gathering the eggs.

بيتر (.m) : ماذا تفعلين؟
beeter: maadha taf°aleen?
Peter: What are you doing?

مريم (.f) : أنا ألعّب الأرنب.
maryam: 'anaa 'ula°ibul-'arnab.
Mariam: I'm petting my rabbit.

Activities نشاطات
nashaaTaat

A

Write the name of each animal in Arabic.

.1 هذه _____.
haadhihi....

.2 هذه _____.
haadhihi....

.3 هذا _____.
haadha....

هذا _____.

haadha....

٤.

هذا _____.

haadha....

٥.

B Identify in Arabic where each animal can be found.

١. المرعى almarʿa

_____

٢. الإسطبل al'isTabl

_____

٣. البركة albirka

_____

٤. الجو aljaw

_____

٥. الزريبة az-zareeba

_____

C Where? Who? What? Which? Circle the correct answer.

٢. أين الحصان؟   ١. أين سامية (.f) وأين محمود (m.)؟
'aynal HiSaan?   'ayna saamiya wa'ayna maHmood?

أ. في الجو fil-jaw   fil-birka في البركة .أ

ب. في الإسطبل fil-'isTabl   fil-marʿa في المرعى .ب

ج. في البركة fil-birka   fir-reef في الريف .ج

3. من معه تفاحة لعلي (.m)؟
mann maʿahu tuffaaHa?

أ. رانية (.f)   raaniya

ب. محمود (.m)   maHmood

ج. الحصان   alHiSaan

4. من يريد أن يساعد؟
mann-yureed 'an yusaaʿid?

أ. رانية   raaniya

ب. محمود   maHmood

ج. أميرة   'ameera

5. ماذا يوجد مع سامية؟
maadha yoojad maʿ saamiya?

أ. بقرة   baqara

ب. عنزة   ʿanza

ج. سطل   saTl

6. أي حيوان هذا؟
'ayy Hayawaan haadha?

أ. الحصان   alHiSaan

ب. العنزة   alʿanza

ج. البقرة   albaqara

D **Complete the sentences by writing the letter of the correct choice.**

1. اسم الهرة _____.
ismul-hirra....

2. الحمار _____.
alHimaar....

3. البقرة في _____.
albaqara fee....

4. التفاحة لـ _____.
attufaHa li....

5. الدجاجة _____.
addajaaja....

أ. كبيرة
kabeera

ب. صغير
Sagheer

ج. رانية (.f)
raaniya

د. المرعى
almarʿa

هـ. سيسي (.f)
seesee

E **Rearrange this group of animals from the smallest to the largest.**

عصفور ʿaSfoor   عنزة ʿanza   أرنب 'arnab   بقرة baqara

1. _____
2. _____
3. _____
4. _____

F
Write the letter of the correct translation of the Arabic sentence.

A. I see the animals.

B. I want to help you.

C. I can gather the eggs.

D. I'm feeding the cat.

E. I can hold the bucket.

F. I am in the country.

١. ــــــــــ أَنا في الريف.
'anaa fir-reef.

٢. ــــــــــ أرى الحيوانات.
'aral-Hayawaanaat.

٣. ــــــــــ أريد أن أساعدك.
'ureedu an 'usaaᶜidaka.

٤. ــــــــــ أستطيع أن أحمل الدلو.
astaTeeᶜu an aHmilad-daloo.

٥. ــــــــــ أطعم الهرة.
'aTᶜamal-hirra.

٦. ــــــــــ أستطيع أن أجمّع البيض.
astaTeeᶜu an 'ujammiᶜal-bayD.

G
لنتكلّم! (*linatakallam!*). **Select four animals from this unit. Ask your speaking partner where each one is. He / she should answer with a logical location. Then, your partner asks you where four other animals are. You answer this time.**

مثال :
mithaal:
Example:

A. أين البطة؟
'aynal-baTTa?

B. في البركة
fil-birka

H
دورك! (*dawrak!*) **Find out whether your classmate knows the names of the animals. Offer a clue for each animal, such as sounds or actions: "It oinks." "It flies." "It gives eggs." Make sure your classmate says الـ (*'al*) before each name. Next, your partner will give you a clue by naming a place, such as a field, pond, stable. You will say in Arabic the name of the animal associated with each place.**

How Do I Write the Arabic Alphabet?

Saad ص and *Daad* ض in the four different positions

Final	Medial	Initial	Independent
ـص	ـصـ	صـ	ص
مقص	قصر	صقر	رصاص
Writing Practice			
ـص	ـصـ	صـ	ص
مقص	قصر	صقر	رصاص

Final	Medial	Initial	Independent
ـض	ـضـ	ضـ	ض
بيض	عضد	ضبع	مرض
Writing Practice			
ـض	ـضـ	ضـ	ض
بيض	عضد	ضبع	مرض

Proverb

" القرد في عين أمه غزال.
alqird fee ʿayn 'ummuh ghazaal.
A monkey is a gazelle in the
eyes of his mother. "

Symtalk

I
In Arabic, write the word or expression that corresponds to each picture.

.4 _____ .3 _____ .2 _____ .1 _____

.7 _____ .6 _____ .5 _____

J
Say and write the question. Then give the answer.

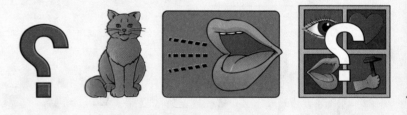

_____ _____

_____ _____

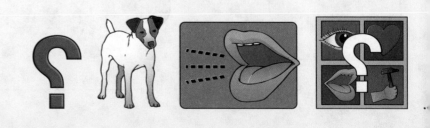

_____ _____

.4

_____   _____

K Work with a partner. After one of you asks the question, the other responds that no, the
person likes a different kind of animal. Then, write the dialogue in Arabic.

.1

_____

_____

.2

_____

_____

.3

_____

_____

.4

_____

_____

.5

_____

_____

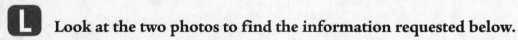

L **Look at the two photos to find the information requested below.**

1. Which animal is the man riding?

   A. حصان
   HiSaan

   B. جمل
   jamal

   C. كلب
   kalb

2. What animals are the two guys watching over?

   A. معزة / ماعز
   maᶜza / maaᶜiz

   B. بقرة / بقر
   baqara / baqar

   C. خروف / خرفان
   kharoof / khurfaan

Unit 8

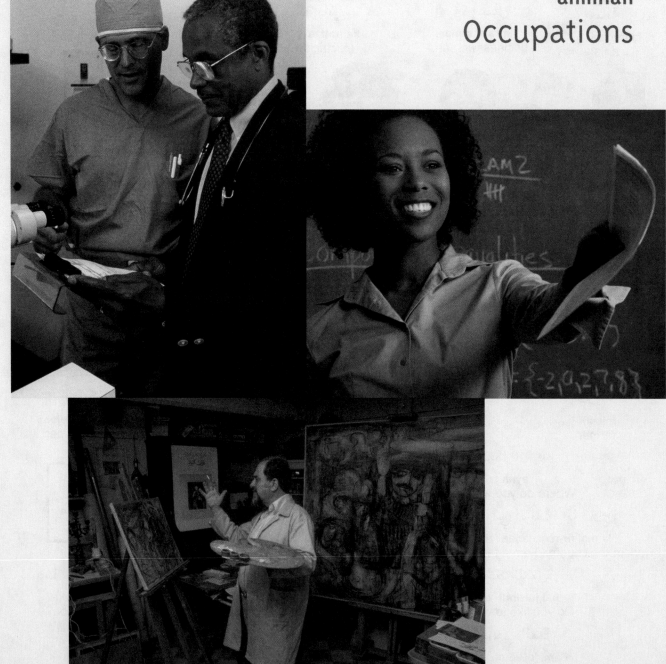

المهن

almihan

Occupations

فنّانة
fannaana
artist

امرأة أعمال
imra'at aᶜmaal
businesswoman

كهربائي
kahrabaa'iy
electrician

نجّار
najjaar
carpenter

طبّاخ
Tabbaakh
cook

طبيب
Tabeeb
physician

ميكانيكي
meekaaneeki
mechanic

ممرّضة
mumarriDa
nurse

موسيقي
mooseeqi
musician

أستاذة
'ustaadha
teacher

فلّاح
fallaaH
farmer

ساعي بريد
saaᶜi bareed
letter carrier

سمكري
samkari
plumber

مبرمج كمبيوتر
mubarmij kumbiyooter
computer programmer

أين تعمل؟
'ayna taᶜmal?
Where do you work?

أعمل في الريف. أنا فلّاح.
'aᶜmal fir-reef. 'anaa fallaaH.
I work in the country. I am a farmer.

هل تحب العمل؟
hal tuHibul-ᶜamal?
Do you like to work?

نعم، أحب العمل.
naᶜam, 'uHibul- ᶜamal.
Yes, I like to work.

Synonyms for "employment" and "work":
waDHeefa وظيفة **shughl** شغل **amal**ᶜ عمل

ماذا تعمل؟
maadhaa taᶜmal?
What do you do (for a living)?

أنا ممثّلة. أعمل في المسرح.
'anaa mumaththila. 'aᶜmal fil-masraH.
I am an actress. I work in the theater.

ما مهنتك؟
maa mihnatuka?
What is your profession?

أنا ممثّل.
'anaa mumaththil.
I am an actor.

A Number the professions or trades in order as your teacher says each one in Arabic.

_____ الكهربائي alkahrabaa'i   _____ الطبيب aTTabeeb

_____ الفلّاح alfallaaH   _____ الميكانيكي almeekaaneeki

_____ الأستاذ al'ustaadh   _____ ساعي البريد saaᶜil-bareed

_____ الموسيقي almooseeqi   _____ الطباخ aTTabbaakh

                                                    _____ التاجر attaajir

B Who works here? Write the name of an appropriate profession or trade.

1. restaurant   _____

2. wood shop   _____

3. post office   _____

4. school   _____

5. auto service station   _____

6. dairy barn   _____

7. stage   _____

8. hospital   _____

9. store   _____

10. office   _____

C Complete the sentences with the Arabic equivalent of the word or expression in parentheses.

1. ما _____؟ (profession)
                   maa...?

2. _____ ممثّل / ممثّلة. (I am)
                   ...mumaththil / mumaththila.

3. _____ في المسرح. (I work)
                   ...fil marsraH.

4. أين _____ يا غسان؟ (m.) (do you work)
                   'ayna... yaa ghassaan?

5. أعمل _____ المطبخ. (in)
'aᶜmal... almaTbakh.

6. ماذا _____؟ (do you do)
maadha...?

7. أنا _____ (cook)
'anaa....

8. _____ أن أعمل. (I like)
...'an 'aᶜmal.

D **Write the sentences in English.**

1. والدتي مترجمة. waalidati mutarjima.

_____

2. تتكلّم الألمانية والبرتغالية. tatakallamul–'almaaniyya walburtughaaliyya.

_____

3. والدي موسيقي. waalidi mooseeqi.

_____

4. يعزف على الجيتار. yaᶜzuf ᶜalal-geetaar.

_____

5. تعمل في الكمبيوتر. taᶜmal fil-kumbiyooter.

_____

6. بنت عمي طباخة. bint ᶜammi Tabbaakha.

_____

7. يحضّر الطعام. yuHaDDiruT-Taᶜaam.

_____

E **Write the name of the profession or occupation in Arabic.**

1. الـ _____ creates software

2. الـ _____ is in charge of healing sick people

3. الـ _____ checks for faulty wiring

4. الـ _____ installs wooden beams

5. الـ _____ paints portraits

6. الـ _____ cooks food

7. الـ _____ manages a company

8. الـ _____ delivers mail

9. الـ _____ plays in a symphony orchestra

F

In Arabic, write the name of the profession or occupation that corresponds to each picture.

1.

_____

2.

_____

3.

_____

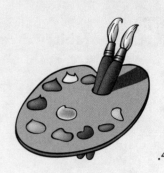

_____ .4

_____ .5

G !لنتكلّم (*linatakallam!*) Guess certain occupations. Give your speaking partner a cue. For example, you say "urgent care" and your partner will say: مستشفى (*mustashfa*). Then he / she gives you a cue, such as "paintbrush" and you will say: فنّان (*fannaan*). Each of you will give five cues to elicit five names of professions or occupations.

H !دورك (*dawrak!*) Help create a classroom bulletin board display about professions and occupations. Cut out pictures from magazines showing people doing the jobs presented in this unit. Label each one in Arabic, for example, هو فنّان (*huwa fannaan*) or هي امرأة أعمال (*hiya 'imra'at 'a⁽maal*). Label the entire display as مهن (*mihan*).

Proverb

" لا تترك عمل اليوم إلى الغد.
laa tatruk ⁽amalul-yawm 'ilal-ghadd.
Don't postpone today's work until tomorrow. **"**

How Do I Write the Arabic Alphabet?

Taa ط and *Dhaa* ظ in the four different positions

Final	Medial	Initial	Independent
ط	ط	ط	ط
مشط	مطر	طير	شوط
Writing Practice			
ـط	ـطـ	طـ	ط
مشط	مطر	طير	شوط

Final	Medial	Initial	Independent
ظ	ظ	ظ	ظ
غيظ	عظم	ظهر	عكاظ
Writing Practice			
ـظ	ـظـ	ظـ	ظ
غيظ	عظم	ظهر	عكاظ

Symtalk

I In Arabic, write the word or expression that corresponds to each picture.

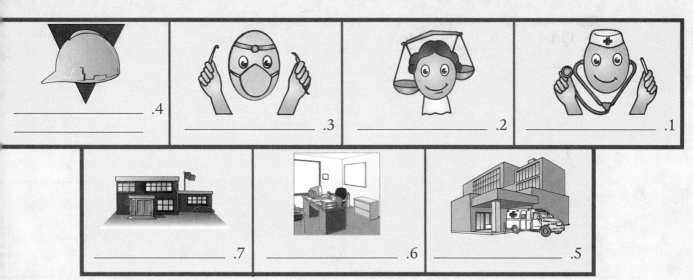

J Say the sentences, then write them in Arabic.

_____

K Work with a partner. Ask the question or give the answer. Then, write the dialogue.

 في

_____   _____

 في

_____   _____

 في

_____   _____

 في

_____   _____

L **Look at the clippings to find the information requested below.**

1. Look at the job ad that starts with مطلوب فورا (*maTloob fawran*) in الإمارات العربية (*al'imaaraatul-ʿarabiyya*) and write in the blank the type of professionals being sought.

_____

2. Circle all the examples of the letters ش ، ص ، ض and in the clippings and write them below in the four different positions:

Final	Medial	Initial	Independent

Unit 9

الطعام

aTTaᶜaam

Food

دكاز خالد
dukkaan khaalid

Khalid's Store
Beverages **muraTTabaat** مرطبات

شوكولاته
shookoolaata
chocolate

خمسة ألاف ليرة/ كيلو
khamsat 'aalaaf leera / keelo
five thousand lira / kilo

حليب
Haleeb
milk

ألف ليرة / لتر
'alf leera / litr
thousand lira / liter

عصير برتقال
ᶜaSeer burtuqaal
orange juice

ثلاثة ألاف ليرة
thalaathat 'aalaaf leera
three thousand lira

ماء
maa'
water

خمس مئة ليرة
khams mi'at leera
five hundred lira

صودا
Sooda
soda

ثماني مئة ليرة
thamaani mi'at leera
eight hundred lira

مطعم أبو نوّاس
maTᶜam abu nawwaas
مأكولات لبنانية
ma'kulaat lubnaaniyya

Abu Nawwaas Restaurant
Lebanese Food

Menu of the day –
Wednesday

الصحن، اليومي – الأربعاء
aSSaHnul-yawmi – al'arbiᶜaa'

فطور
futoor

Breakfast

1. فول مدمّس مع البصل والنعناع وفنجان قهوة
fool mudammas maᶜal-baSal wannaᶜnaaᶜ wafinjaan qahwa

1. Marinated fava beans with onions, mint, and a cup of coffee

2. مناقيش زعتر ولحم بعجين وفطاير بالجبنة مع فنجان شاي
manaaqeesh zaᶜtar walaHim biᶜajeen wafataayir biljubna maᶜ finjaan shaay

2. Zaatar pita, meat pita, and cheese pie, with a cup of tea

مأكولات فاخرة!
ma'koolaat faakhira!

Quality food!

هناك حليب.	ماذا يوجد هناك للشرب؟	هناك شوربة وسلاطة.	ماذا يوجد هناكَ للأكل؟
hunaaka Haleeb.	**maadha yoojad hunaaka lishshurb?**	**hunaaka shoorba wasalaaTa.**	**maadha yoojad hunaaka lil'akl?**
There's milk.	What is there to drink?	There's soup and salad.	What's there to eat?

لا، أنا لست عطشان.	هل أنت عطشان يا شادي؟	نعم أنا جوعان.	هل أنت جوعان؟
laa, 'anaa lastu ᶜaTshaan.	**hal 'anta ᶜaTshaan yaa shady?**	**naᶜam, 'anaa jawᶜaan.**	**hal 'anta jawᶜaan?**
No, I'm not thirsty.	Are you thirsty, Shadi?	Yes, I'm hungry.	Are you hungry?

أنا أشرب كباية حليب.	ماذا تشربين يا سميرة؟	أنا آكل سندويش.	ماذا تأكلين (f.)؟ / ماذا تأكل (m.)؟
'anaa 'ashrab kubbaayat Haleeb.	**madhaa tashrabeen yaa sameera?**	**'anaa 'aakul sandweesh.**	**maadha ta'kuleen? / maadha ta'kul?**
I'm drinking a glass of milk.	What are you drinking, Samira?	I'm eating a sandwich.	What are you eating?

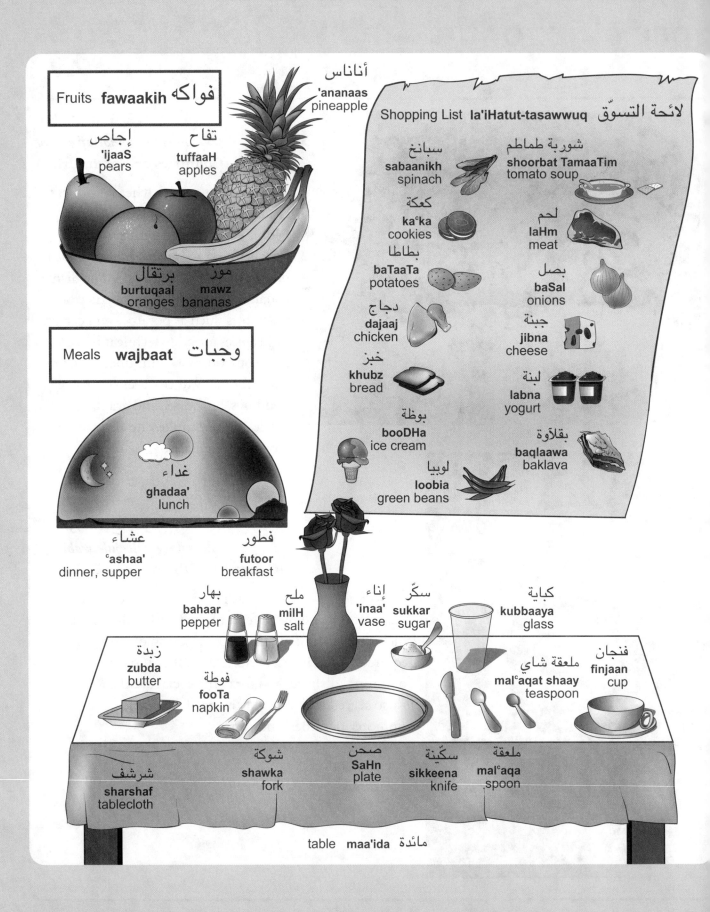

Fruits **fawaakih** فواكه

أناناس
'ananaas
pineapple

إجاص
'ijaaS
pears

تفاح
tuffaaH
apples

برتقال
burtuqaal
oranges

موز
mawz
bananas

Shopping List **la'iHatut-tasawwuq** لائحة التسوّق

سبانخ
sabaanikh
spinach

شوربة طماطم
shoorbat TamaaTim
tomato soup

كعكة
ka°ka
cookies

لحم
laHm
meat

بطاطا
baTaaTa
potatoes

بصل
baSal
onions

دجاج
dajaaj
chicken

جبنة
jibna
cheese

خبز
khubz
bread

لبنة
labna
yogurt

بوظة
booDHa
ice cream

بقلآوة
baqlaawa
baklava

لوبيا
loobia
green beans

Meals **wajbaat** وجبات

غداء
ghadaa'
lunch

عشاء
°ashaa'
dinner, supper

فطور
futoor
breakfast

بهار
bahaar
pepper

ملح
milH
salt

إناء
'inaa'
vase

سكّر
sukkar
sugar

كباية
kubbaaya
glass

فنجان
finjaan
cup

زبدة
zubda
butter

فوطة
fooTa
napkin

ملعقة شاي
mal°aqat shaay
teaspoon

شرشف
sharshaf
tablecloth

شوكة
shawka
fork

صحن
SaHn
plate

سكّينة
sikkeena
knife

ملعقة
mal°aqa
spoon

table **maa'ida** مائدة

Specialties of the Arab World

دول شمال أفريقيا
duwal shamaal'afreeqiya
(Countries of North Africa)

■ كسكس Couscous, a wheat product, is a famous dish from North Africa. People eat it topped with دجاج *dajaaj* (chicken), لحم غنم *laHm ghanam* (lamb), or لحم بقر *laHm baqar* (beef). The dish is usually accompanied by a medley of vegetables, such as potatoes and carrots. Mild spices are added while it is cooking. Couscous is a communal dish, prepared for many festive events, such as weddings, birthdays, and graduation parties. Some families, however, prepare it on a regular basis.

دول الخليج العربي
duwalul-khaleejul-ʿarabi
(Countries of the Arabian Gulf)

■ كبسة *Kabsa* is a famous dish from the gulf region of Arabia. It is a rice-based feast topped with either lamb, chicken, or fish. A balanced combination of spices is required to produce a perfect *kabsa*. It is another communal dish, cooked for many social events. *Kabsa* is also served with an assortment of vegetables, such as onions, potatoes, and carrots.

دول الهلال الخصيب
duwalul-hilaalul-khaSeeb
(Fertile Crescent Countries)

■ كبه *Kibbi* is a famous dish from the Fertile Crescent region of the Arab world, namely لبنان *lubnaan*. It is prepared by finely tenderizing meat— fatless beef or lamb mixed with برغل *burghul* (cracked wheat) and light spices, such as allspice and white pepper. *Kibbi* is prepared in many different ways. It may be in the form of patties stuffed with walnuts and pine nuts, or spread in a pan in two layers with a sauteed onion and ground meat stuffing between the layers. It is also served raw or sautéed and eaten with Arab bread.

■ فلافل *Falaafil* is a famous dish in all regions of the Arab world. It is a vegetable burger made of فول *fool* (fava beans), and حمص *HummuS* (garbanzo beans). Parsley and spices are added to the mix. *Falaafil* is deep-fried in vegetable oil until the color of the patties is dark brown. Eaten with خبز *khubz*, Arab bread, it is often dipped in طحينة *TaHeena* (sesame dip) and topped with mixed vegetables such as lettuce, pickled turnips, tomato, mint, and parsley.

■ صحتين (*SaHtayn*) is an expression used to wish someone a happy and / or healthy meal.

■ مأكول الهناء (*ma'koolul-hanaa'*) is another popular and more formal expression used to express "Enjoy your meal."

■ حليب (*Haleeb*) is the word for milk in Lebanon and some other neighboring Arab countries. لبن (*laban*) is another word used for milk in Egypt and some other places in North Africa.

■ In Egypt فلافل (*falaafil*) is called طعميّة (*Tu'miyya*).

A Write the Arabic name of each object.

_____ .1

_____ .2

_____ .3

_____ .4

_____

_____

_____

_____

B **Complete each sentence in English.**

1. كبسه is a dish prepared mainly in _____

2. What are the two main ingredients used to make فلافل? _____.

3. Which country in particular is famous for كبه? _____.

4. What kind of meat is used for كسكس? _____.

5. What is بقلاوة? _____

C **Using your food vocabulary and the list of specialties, write three food items for each of the following categories.**

1. **meat**

   A. _____

   B. _____

   C. _____

2. **vegetables**

   A. _____

   B. _____

   C. _____

3. **dairy products**

   A. _____

   B. _____

   C. _____

4. **beverages**

   A. _____

   B. _____

   C. _____

5. **fruits**

A. _____

B. _____

C. _____

6. **desserts**

A. _____

B. _____

C. _____

D Imagine you are opening a restaurant in Saudi Arabia. From your food and specialty lists, prepare a menu for lunch and dinner. At least three dishes or items for each meal should be offered.

E Prepare a poster using magazine pictures. Show a balanced breakfast and a balanced dinner. Label each food item with its Arabic name.

F Prepare 15 different flash cards with a picture of a food item on one side and its Arabic name on the other. Select several of your flash cards and quiz a few classmates.

G Play this game with a group that includes several of your classmates. List in Arabic 20 words for foods or beverages. Then, scramble each word. The student who unscrambles the most words correctly in the time allotted is the winner.

H لنتكلّم! (*linatakallam!*) Your classmate is in charge of the menu today. In Arabic, tell him or her that you are hungry. You want to know what there is to eat today. Your partner will name five foods and you will pick one. Next, your partner will tell you that he or she is thirsty and ask you what there is to drink. Name five beverages so that your partner can pick one.

I دورك! (*dawrak!*) Imagine that you work at a very nice restaurant in Kuwait. A customer asks you about a regional specialty, such as *kabsa*. Explain what this specialty is and how it is made.

Proverb

الجائع يحلم بفرن الخبز. **"**
aljaa'iᶜ yaHlam bifurnal-khubz.
The hungry dream of a bread bakery. **"**

How Do I Write the Arabic Alphabet?

ᶜayn ع and *ghayn* غ in the four different positions

Final	Medial	Initial	Independent
ـع	ـعـ	عـ	ع
سلع	نعل	عنب	قاع
Writing Practice			
ـع	ـعـ	عـ	ع
بسلع	نعل	عنب	قاع

Final	Medial	Initial	Independent
ـغ	ـغـ	غـ	غ
رسغ	بغل	غرب	صاغ
Writing Practice			
ـغ	ـغـ	غـ	غ
رسغ	بغل	غرب	صاغ

Symtalk

J   In the space, write the correct word or expression in Arabic.

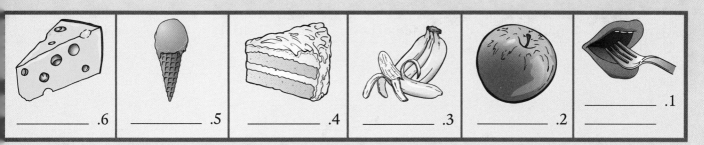

.6 _____   .5 _____   .4 _____   .3 _____   .2 _____   .1 _____

K   Say the sentences, then write them.

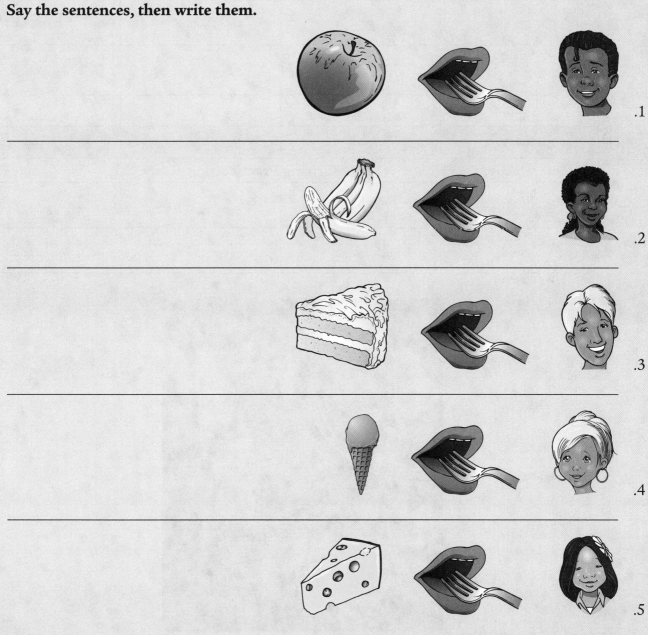

L **Work with a partner. Ask the question or give the answer. Then, write the dialogue.**

.1

.2

.3

.4

.5

M **Look at the clippings to find the information requested below.**

1. A. What is the name of the restaurant that serves hamburgers?

    _____

    B. What kind of dessert is available from the bakery?

    _____

2. Circle all the examples of the letter ع and two other letters that you recognize in the clippings and write them below in the four different positions:

Final	Medial	Initial	Independent

Unit 10

الفن
alfann
Art

Vocabulary المفردات

almufradaat

خطوط عربية
khuTooT ᶜarabiyya
calligraphy

خطاط
khaTTaaT
calligrapher

رسام
rassaam
painter

لوحة
lawHa
painting

نحّات
naHHaat
sculptor

تمثال
timthaal
sculpture

فنان
fannaan
artist

خريطة
khareeTa
map

مهندس معماري
muhandis mᶜmaari
architect

Modern Arab art developed as a result of the interaction between the colonial powers of the West and the Middle East. Easel painting is a recent phenomenon that started in the early 20th century. The first official school of fine art was the School of Fine Arts in Cairo, opened in 1908 by Prince Yusuf Kamal. Modern painting from the Arab world embraced the Western styles of landscape painting and abstract painting. The emerging Arab artists wanted to honor their creative heritage by combining techniques of the West with the cultural values of the Middle East. The old art of calligraphy is still used in modern paintings. Arab art of the 20th century uses Western methods but expresses common Arab sentiments and issues. The politics of the Middle East is reflected on the pages of many Arab artists' works. The Arab world does not have world-famous artists like Picasso, Monet, or Van Gogh. However, there are a number of artists who made significant contributions to the field, such as Wijdan Ali from Jordan, Sliman Mansour and Kamal Boullata from Palestine, Mahmoud Said from Egypt, and Joseph Matar from Lebanon. In addition, famous monuments and structures built by

Kingdom Tower in Riyadh, Saudi Arabia

great Arab engineers, designed by notable architects, and decorated by brilliant mosaic layers and calligraphers are found in all quarters of the Arab world.

Calligraphy خطوط يدوية عربية

khuTooT yadawiyya ᶜarabiyya

Calligraphy is considered one of the most important art forms in the Islamic world. It is prized more than painting and other visual arts. Since the *qur'aan* (القرآن) was written using highly stylized forms of decorative calligraphy, the art itself has come to be revered as a sacred art. The practice of calligraphy

allowed artists to work creatively without portraying figural images. Some followers of mystical branches of Islam use calligraphy in the form of calligrams to hide images of sacred people and animals. It can take hours to figure out the meaning hidden within an Arabic letter. Numerous forms of calligraphy are used for different purposes. The *kufic* (الكوفي) script is formal and uses broad and angular letters; it is usually used on public monuments. The *naskh* (النسخ) script is the cursive style that children in the Arab world learn to use for writing and learning. Featuring broad rounded letters with adequate spacing,

Can you identify any Arabic letters in this calligraphy?

it is also the script used throughout this book. This style is most commonly seen in the *qur'aan* and in printed material. The *diwaani* (الديواني) style was popular during the time of the Ottoman Turkish Empire. It is characterized by complex lines and letters placed closely together. This style required a great deal of education in order to read. The *raqᶜa* (رقعة) style of calligraphy is easy to read and requires minimal effort to write. The letters in this style are simple and concise. Arabic calligraphy is also used to attract attention. Today it's used on store banners, newspaper advertisements, as well as huge billboard signs. Ahmad Abdul Fattah al-Bashli from Egypt is considered among the top calligraphers of the modern era.

Dome of the Rock Mosque جامع قبة الصخره

jaami ᶜqubbatuS-Sakhara

The Dome of the Rock is a mosque located in Jerusalem. Built in 691 A.D. by the *Umayyad aliph Abdul Malik bin Marwan*, it is one of the oldest and most enduring of Islamic structures. It was constructed to reflect the glory of the Islamic culture and civilization and was built in the same place where the Jewish Temple had stood until 70 A.D. The rock over which the mosque was built is said to be the place where Abraham had prepared to sacrifice his son *Ismaᶜil* to God. It is also the place that Muslims believe the Prophet

The Dome of the Rock is one of the most popular landmarks in Jerusalem.

Mohammed ascended to heaven in a journey called the **miʿraaj** (المعراج). The interior of the mosque is a circle enclosed within a series of octagonal shapes. The walls are decorated in blue, green, and mother-of-pearl ceramic tiles. The designs do not contain any animal or human figures, which would be a violation of Islamic artistic tradition. This mosque was ground-breaking in design, because all of the structural details like brick and stone were covered up in marble tiles. Like all mosques, the Dome of the Rock has a prayer area, or *miHraab*. The *miHraab* has a shape of a niche. It simply indicates the *qiblah*, which is the direction of Mecca. The interior walls are also decorated with Arabic calligraphy taken from the *qur'aan*.

Beit Eddin Palace قصر بيت الدينُ

qaSr baytud-deer

A magnificent palace located about 25 miles east of Beirut in the Shouf Mountains, Beit Eddin was built in the early 19th century and took three decades to complete. It is the most famous architectural landmark in Lebanon. Built for the ruler of Mount Lebanon, Emir Bashir II, the palace interior is decorated with mosaics and stone engraving. The walls and ceiling are filled with Arabic inscriptions and calligraphy. It has multiple glass-studded

Today the Palace houses a museum of feudal weapons, costumes, and jewelry, as well as an archeological museum and a museum of Byzantine mosaics.

cupolas in its fancy Turkish baths. There are three living quarters that were used by the Emir and his family. Beit Eddin Palace also has a guest house and a huge courtyard with colonnades and water jets and fountains. It overlooks the valley of *Dayral-Qamar*. Today the palace is a national antiquity site. It has a museum, which displays folkloric items from 19th-century Lebanon, as well as antiquities and mosaics that date back to the Byzantine era. The Palace is also famous for its **International Festival** (مهرجانات بيت الدين) that takes place in its vast courtyard. The festival attracts entertainers from all over the world. It is one of the most popular tourist sites in Lebanon.

A   **Name the object or person that...**

1. is known for its magnificent dome.

    _____

2. has multiple script writing.

    _____

3. is located in the mountains of Lebanon.

    _____

4. opened in 1908.

    _____

5. is an area in a mosque built in the direction of Mecca.

    _____

B   **Write the name of the person who...**

1. ... draws blue prints.

    _____

2. ... make sculptures.

    _____

3. ... draws paintings.

    _____

4. ... writes calligraphy.

    _____

5. ... practices an art as a vocation.

    _____

C Match the word or phrase from column A with a related word from column B.

B	A
أ. القاهرة alqaahira	1. خريطة _____ khareeTa
ب. خط يدوي عربي khaTT yadawi ʿarabi	2. لوحة _____ lawHa
ج. نحّات naHHaat	3. تمثال _____ timthaal
د. فنّان fannaan	4. مدرسة الفنون الجميلة _____ madrasatul-funoonul-jameela
هـ. مهندس muhandis	5. نسخ _____ naskh
و. قبة الصخرة qubbatuS-Sakhra	6. معراج _____ miʿraaj
ز. رسّام rassaam	7. فن _____ fann

D Complete the analogies.

1. رسام: لوحة = خطاط: _____ <br> rassaam: lawHa = khaTTaaT: ….

2. _____ : خريطة = نحات: تمثال
 …. : khareeTa = naHHaat: timthaal

3. قرآن: سور = _____ : قبلة
 Qur'aan: suwar = …. : qibla

4. _____ : فن = رسم: رسامة <br> fann: …. = rasm: rassaama

E **Match the picture cue with the name of the building or art form.**

A.

1. ـــــــــ قصر بيت الدين
qaSr baytud-deen

B.

2. ـــــــــ خطوط عربية
khuTooT ᶜarabiyya

C.

3. ـــــــــ قبة الصخرة
qubbatuS-Sakhra

F **What is the Arabic name of . . .**

1. … cursive connected Arabic letters?

   _____

2. … a famous decorated dome?

   _____

3. … a palace that has a courtyard overlooking a valley?

   _____

4. … summer festivities that take place in a palace courtyard?

   _____

5. … modern art?

   _____

G Which of the art forms or buildings or architectural styles in this unit do you like best? State in your own words why you like it.

_____

_____

_____

_____

_____

_____

_____

H Read the dialogues aloud with a partner.

حسام (m.): هل تحب الفن العربي؟
Husaam: hal tuHibbul-fannul-ᶜarabi?
Husaam: Do you like Arabic art?

سعيد (m.): نعم أحب الخط العربي كثيرا.
saᶜeed: naᶜam 'uHibul-khaTul-ᶜarabi katheeran.
Saeed: Yes, I like Arabic calligraphy a lot.

حسّان (m.): هل هذا جامع؟
Hassaan: hal haadha jaamiᶜ?
Hasaan: Is this a mosque?

منى (f.): لا هذا قصر.
muna: laa, haadha qaSr.
Mona: No, this is a palace.

I دورك! (*dawrak!*) Look at the following calligraphy styles and try to identify the letters that you know and read the sentence.

نسخ naskh

أنا طالب في مدرسة ابتدائية وأختي طالبة في مدرسة إعدادية وابنة عمي أستاذة في مدرسة ثانوية

deewaany ديواني

أنا طالب في مدرسة ابتدائية وأختي طالبة في مدرسة إعدادية وابنة عمي أستاذة في مدرسة ثانوية

koofi كوفي

أنا طالب في مدرسة ابتدائية وأختي طالبة في مدرسة إعدادية وابنة عمي أستاذة في مدرسة ثانوية

مدير mudeer

أنا طالب في مدرسة ابتدائية وأختي طالبة في مدرسة إعدادية وابنة عمي أستاذة في مدرسة ثانوية

أندلسي andalusy

أنا طالب في مدرسة ابتدائية وأختي طالبة في مدرسة إعدادية وابنة عمي أستاذة في مدرسة ثانوية

Write the English equivalent of the sentence here:

_____

_____

_____

_____

Proverb

" العبرة بالأعمال وليست بالأقوال.
al'ibra bil'a'maal walaysat bil'aqwaal.
Action speaks louder than words. **"**

How Do I Write the Arabic Alphabet?

faa ف and *qaaf* ق in the four positions

Final	Medial	Initial	Independent
ف	ـفـ	فـ	ف
صيف	صفر	فرو	رف
Writing Practice			

Final	Medial	Initial	Independent
ـق	ـقـ	قـ	ق
دبق	بقر	قدم	ساق
Writing Practice			

Symtalk

J In the space, write the correct word or expression in Arabic.

_____ .4	_____ .3	_____ .2	_____ .1
_____ .8	_____ .7	_____ .6	_____ .5

K Say the sentences, then write them.

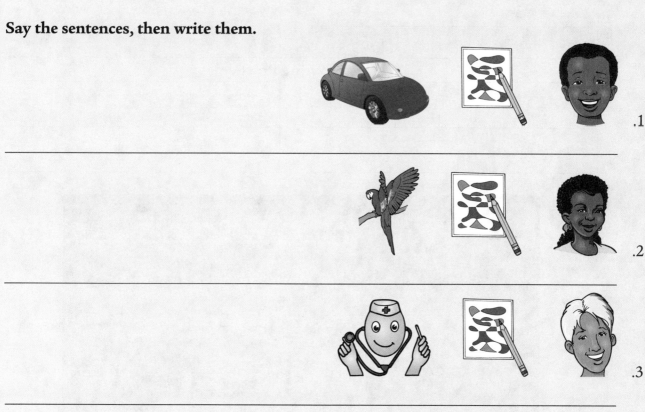

.1

_____

.2

_____

.3

_____

.4

_____

.5

_____

L **Work with a partner. Ask the question or give the answer. Then, write the dialogue.**

_____

.1

_____

.2

_____

.3

_____

_____

.4

_____

_____

.5

_____

Living Language لغتنا الحيّة

lughatunal-Hayya

M **Look at the clippings to find the information requested below.**

1. A. The two clippings represent an advertisement for a festival of poetry and a musical. Which word means "poetry"?

   _____

   B. Which word means "musical"?

   _____

2. Circle all the examples of the letters ق ، ف ، غ ، and ط in the clippings and write them below in the four positions:

Final	Medial	Initial	Independent

Unit 11

الجسم والصحة

aljism waSSiHHa

Body and Health

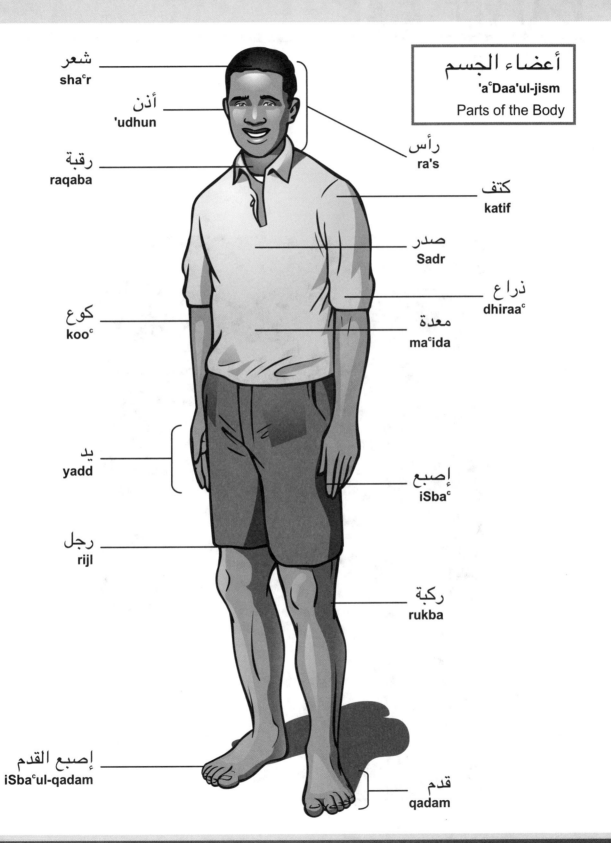

أعضاء الجسم

'aᶜDaa'ul-jism

Parts of the Body

شعر
shaᶜr

أذن
'udhun

رقبة
raqaba

كوع
kooᶜ

يد
yadd

رجل
rijl

إصبع القدم
iSbaᶜul-qadam

رأس
ra's

كتف
katif

صدر
Sadr

ذراع
dhiraaᶜ

معدة
maᶜida

إصبع
iSbaᶜ

ركبة
rukba

قدم
qadam

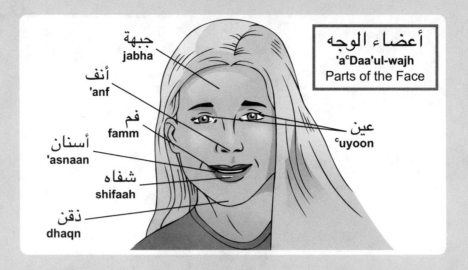

أعضاء الوجه
'aᶜDaa'ul-wajh
Parts of the Face

جبهة
jabha

أنف
'anf

فم
famm

أسنان
'asnaan

شفاه
shifaah

ذقن
dhaqn

عين
ᶜuyoon

مفردات إضافيّة Extra Vocabulary

mufradaat iDaafiyya

صحة	بخير	مضطرب
SiHHa	**bikhayr**	**muDTarib**
health	well	feeling bad

صحي	مريض	حزين	سعيد
SiHHi	**mareeD**	**Hazeen**	**saᶜeed**
healthy	sick, ill	sad	happy

فرح (m.): مرحبا، كيف حالكِ يا فيروز؟
faraH: marHaba, kayfa Haaluki yaa fayrooz?
Farah: Hi, Fairouz. How are you?

فيروز (f.): لستُ بخير، أنا مضطربة.
fayrooz: lastu bikhayr. 'anaa muDTariba.
Fayruz: I'm not doing well. I feel bad.

مكرم (m.): هل تعمل كثيرا؟
makram: hal taᶜmal katheeran?
Makram: Are you working a lot?

رمزي (m.): لا، أنا أدرس للإمتحان.
ramzy: laa, 'anaa 'adrus lil'imtiHaan.
Ramzi: No, I'm just studying for a test.

وفيقة (f.): ما بكَ؟
wafeeqa: maa bika?
Wafiqa: What's the matter?

مروان (m.): عندي صداع.
marwan: ᶜindi Sudaaᶜ.
Marwan: I've got a headache.

أسعد (m.): هل أمال (f.) مريضة اليوم؟
'asᶜad: hal 'amaal mareeDal-yawm?
Asad: Is Amaal sick today?

كاشي (f.): نعم، معها انفلونزا.
kaathy: naᶜam, maᶜaha infloowanza.
Kathy: Yes, she has the flu.

جوي (m.): كيف تشعر؟
jowy: kayfa tashᶜur?
Joey: How do you feel?

شربل (m.): أنا بخير.
sharbil: 'anaa bikhayr.
Sharbil: I'm feeling good.

جيمي (m.): هل أنت حزينة يا (f.) سيمون؟
jimiy: hal 'anti Hazeena yaa siymoon?
Jimmy: Simone, are you sad?

سيمون (f.): لا. أنا سعيدة.
seemoon: laa, 'anaa saᶜeeda.
Simone: No. I am happy.

A Label the parts of the body in Arabic.

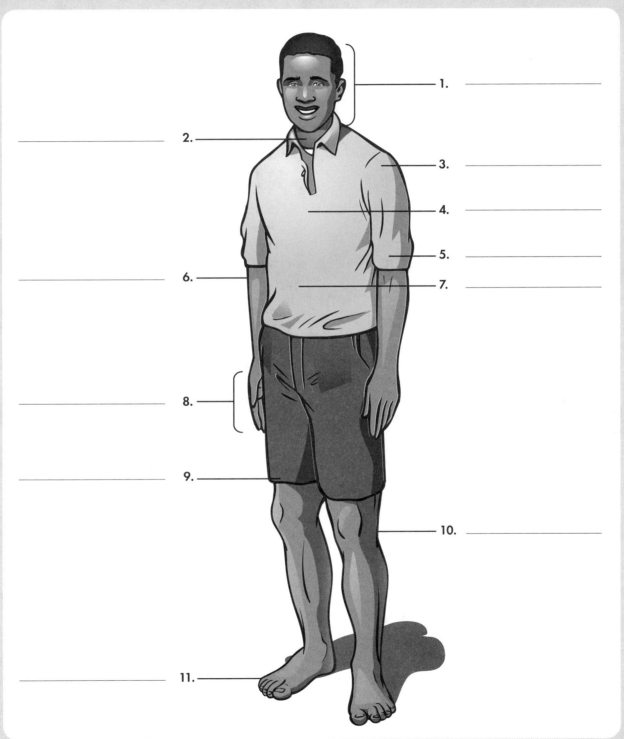

1. _____
2. _____
3. _____
4. _____
5. _____
6. _____
7. _____
8. _____
9. _____
10. _____
11. _____

B Label the parts of the face in Arabic.

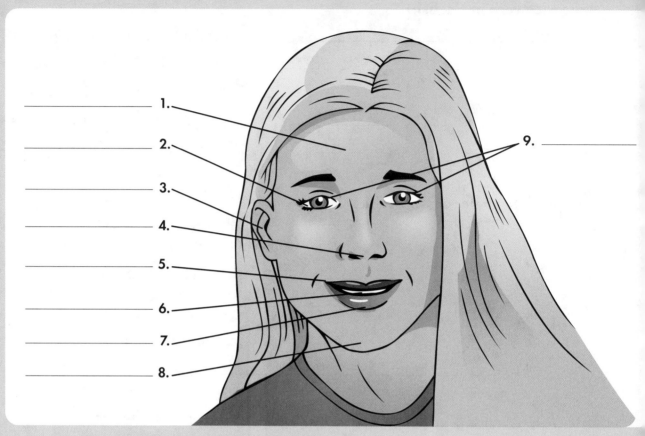

1. _____
2. _____
3. _____
4. _____
5. _____
6. _____
7. _____
8. _____
9. _____

C Complete each sentence with a word in Arabic.

1. We see with our _____

2. To speak I open my _____

3. An _____ is necessary to hear.

4. You hold your pen in your _____

5. Your _____ are needed to bite and chew food.

6. One _____ has five toes.

7. We use the _____ to smell a rose.

8. We play the guitar with our _____

9. The "funny bone" is located on the _____

10. If you eat too much, your _____ will hurt.

D What do you do with your senses? Guess the meaning of the verbs in each sentence. Then write each verb in English.

1. أنا أتكلّم من فمي. anaa atakallam min famy. _____

2. أنا ألمس بأصابعي. anaa almus bi'aSaabiᶜy. _____

3. أنا أرى بعيوني. anaa ara biᶜuyoony. _____

4. أنا أسمع بأذنيّ. anaa asmaᶜ bi'udhunay. _____

5. أنا أشمّ بأنفي. anaa ashumm bi'anfy. _____

E Complete the dialogues in Arabic.

1. محمّد (m.): muHammad:
كيف تشعرين يا ريما؟
kayfa tashᶜureen ya reema?

ريما (f.): reema:
أنا _____ (bad)
'anaa....

2. فارس (m.): faaris:
كيف حالك يا يوسف؟
kayfa Haluka ya yoosuf?

يوسف (m.): yoosuf:
أنا _____ (well)
'anaa....

3. شلبي (f.): shalbi:
هل مايا معها انفلونزا؟
hal maaya maᶜaha infloowanza?

أليشا (f.): 'aleesha:
نعم، هي _____ (sick)
naᶜam, hiya....

4. لبيبة (f.): labeeba:
هل أنت حزين؟
hal 'antaa Hazeen?

قاسم (m.): qaasim:
لا أنا _____ (happy)
laa, 'anaa....

F In Arabic, name the part of the body associated with each illustration.

_____ 1.

_____ 2.

_____ .3

_____ .4

_____ .5

_____ .6

_____ .7

_____ 8.

_____ 9.

_____ 10.

G **Match each part of the body on the right to the activity associated with it on the left.**

A. running

B. smelling

C. carrying

D. listening

E. seeing

F. thinking

G. digesting

H. writing

I. touching

J. speaking

_____ 1. يد yadd

_____ 2. قدم qadam

_____ 3. عيون ᶜuyoon

_____ 4. أنف 'anf

_____ 5. أذنان 'udhunaan

_____ 6. معدة maᶜida

_____ 7. فم famm

_____ 8. ذراع dhiraaᶜ

_____ 9. رأس ra's

_____ 10. إصبع iSbaᶜ

Read the paragraph. Choose the correct answers based on your reading.

اسمي أليشا (f.). عمري عشر سنوات. أنا بخير وبصحّة جيّدة. أفكر من رأسي.
'ismi 'aleesha. ʿumri ʿashar sanawaat. 'anaa bikhayr wabiSiHHa jayyida. 'ufakkir min ra'si.

أتكلّم العربية من فمي. أكتب بيدي وأمشي إلى المدرسة على قدماي.
'atakallamul-ʿarabiyya min fami. 'aktub biyadi wa'amshi 'ilal-madrasa ʿala qadamaay.

أشمّ الزهور في الحديقة من أنفي. أمضغ طعامي بأسناني.
'ashummuz-zuhoor fil-Hadeeqa min 'anfi. 'amDagh Taʿaami bi'asnaani.

مع	ma	with	أمشي	'amshi	I walk	أمضغ	'amDugh	I chew
أظنّ	'aDHunn	I think	أشمّ	'ashumm	I smell			

٤. أليشا، على قدميها....
'aleesha, ʿala qadamayha....
أ. تمشي إلى المدرسة tamshy 'ilal madrasa
ب. تكتب إلى هشام taktubu 'ila hishaam
ج. تلمس القلم talmusul-qalam
هـ. تشمّ الزهور tashummuz-zuhoor

٥. أليشا هي... جداً.
'aleesha hiya... jiddan.
أ. حزينة Hazeena
ب. سعيدة saʿeeda
ج. مضطربة muDTariba
هـ. مريضة mareeDa

١. أليشا (f.) هي....
'aleesha hiya....
أ. بنت bint
ب. رجل rajul
ج. ولد walad
هـ. امرأة imra'a

٢. أليشا عمرها....
'aleesha ʿumruha....
أ. إحدى عشر 'iHda ʿashar
ب. تسعة tisʿa
ج. إثنا عشر 'ithnaa ʿashar
هـ. عشرة ʿashara

٣. أليشا تتكلّم من....
'aleesha tatakallam min....
أ. يدها yadiha
ب. قدمها qadamiha
ج. فمها famiha
هـ. أذنها 'udhuniha

I لنتكلّم! (*linatakallam!*) **Ask your classmate in Arabic where a part of the body is. Your classmate will point to a part of the body. Take turns until you have identified ten parts of the body.**

	مثال:
	mithaal:
	Example:
Where is the nose?	'aynal-'anf?	A: أين الأنف؟
Here is the nose.	haadha huwal-'anf.	B: هذا هو الأنف.

J دورك! (*dawrak!*) Find magazine pictures showing people in different states of health or well-being. Paste these pictures on a poster and write a caption about each one. For example, under a picture of a girl with a cold, write هي مريضة (*hiya mareeDa*) or معها انفلونزا (*maʿaha infloowanza*). Under the picture of a boy playing, write هو سعيد (*huwa saʿeed*).

Proverb

> **العقل السليم في الجسم السليم**
> **alʿaqlus-saleem fil-jismis-saleem**
> A healthy mind is in a healthy body.

How Do I Write the Arabic Alphabet?

kaaf ك and *laam* ل in the four different positions

Final	Medial	Initial	Independent
ك	ـكـ	كـ	ك
ملك	سكّر	كتاب	شباك
Writing Practice			

Final	Medial	Initial	Independent
ـل	ـلـ	لـ	ل
عسل	فلك	لون	مال
Writing Practice			

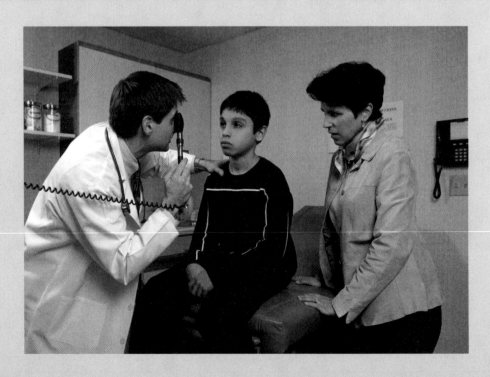

Symtalk

K In the space, write the correct word or expression in Arabic.

4. _____   3. _____   2. _____   1. _____

7. _____   6. _____   5. _____

L Say the sentences, then write them in Arabic.

.1

_____

.2

_____

.3

_____

.4

_____

.5

_____

 **Work with a partner. Ask the question or give the answer. Then, write the dialogue.**

.1

_____

.2

_____

.3

_____

.4

_____

Look at the clippings to find the information requested below.

1. A. What does the clipping with the heart advise you to do on a daily basis?

   _____

   B. The mountain clipping talks about a product. In which country is the product sold?

   _____

2. Circle the letters ل and ك in the clippings and write them below in the four positions:

Final	Medial	Initial	Independent

Unit 12

155

Vocabulary المفردات

almufradaat

ملبوسات رجّالية
malboosaat rijjaaliyya
Men's Clothing

ملبوسات نسائية
malboosaat nisaa'iyya
Women's Clothing

بيجامة (f.) **beejaama**

كنزة (f.) **kanza**

بذلة (f.) **badhla**

قميص (m.) **qameeS**

ربطة عنق (f.) **rabTat ᶜunq**

منديل (m.) **mandeel**

banTaloon بنطلون (m.)

سترة (f.) / جاكيت (m.) **sitra/jakeet**

حذاء (m.) **Hidhaa'**

كلسات (f.) **kalsaat**

كفوف (m.) **kufoof**

ثوب الحمام (m.) **thawbul-Hammaam**

بيجامة (f.) **beejaama**

فستان (m.) **fustaan**

قبعة (f.) **qubbaᶜa**

بلوزة حرير (f.) **blooza Hareer**

سير (m.) **sayr**

تنورة (f.) **tannoora**

حذاء تنس (m.) **Hidhaa' tanis**

حذاء كعب عالي (m.) **Hidhaa' kaᶜb ᶜaali**

وليد (m.): ماذا تلبس؟
waleed: maadha talbus?
Walid: What are you wearing?

خالد (m.): ألبس بذلتي الجديدة.
khaalid: 'albus badhlatil-jadeeda.
Khalid: I'm wearing my new suit.

وليد: لماذا؟
waleed: limaadha?
Walid: Why?

خالد: لأنني ذاهبا إلى الحفلة الموسيقية هذا المساء.
khaalid: li'annani dhahiban 'ilal-Haflal-museeqiyya haadhal-masaa'.
Khalid: Because I'm going to a concert this evening.

كمال (m.): أنا خارج إلى الحديقة.
kamal: 'anaa kharij 'ilal-Hadeeqa.
Kamal: I'm going out to the garden.

رويدا (f.): انتظرني. أنا خارجة معك. سأبحث على سترتي أولا.
ruwayda: intaDHirni. 'anaa kharija maᶜaka. sa'abHath ᶜala sitrati 'awalan.
Rowayda: Wait for me. I'm going with you. But first I'm going to look for my jacket.

قبعة بيسبول (قلوسة) (.f)
qubba°t baysbool (qalloosa)

بلوز (.f)
blooz

جينز (.m)
jeenz

شورت (.m)
shoort

ميّو (.m)
mayyo

شورت (.m)
shoort

جينز (.m)
jeenz

شورت سباحة (.m)
shoort sibaaHa

سميرة (.f) sameera

إجازة الشتاء
'ijaazatush-shitaa'
Winter vacation

جبل لبنان – شباط
jabal lubnaan - shubaaT
Mount Lebanon – February

ثلاثة بنطلونات thalaathat banTaloonaat	سترة sitra
ثلاثة قمصان thalaathat qumSaan	كنزة kanza
ثلاث قبعات thalaath qubba°aat	بلوزتان bloozataan
	تنورة tannoora
ثلاثة مناديل thalaathat manaadeel	كفوف kufoof
	فستانان fustaanaan
	بيجاما beejaama
	سيران sayraan
	كلسات kalsaat

عبير (.f): كيف هذا المعطف؟
°abeer: kayfa haadhal-mi°Taf?
Abir: How's this coat?

فارس (.m): هو جميل جدا.
faaris: huwa jameel jiddan.
Faris: It's very pretty.

أنيس (.m): ماذا تفعلين يا سميرة؟
'anees: maadha taf°aleen ya sameera?
Anis: What are you doing, Samira?

سميرة (.f): أجهّز حقائبي.
sameera: 'ujahhiz Haqaa'ibi.
Samira: I'm packing my suitcase.

أنيس: لماذا؟
'anees: limaadha?
Anis: Why?

سميرة: لأني مسافرة إلى جبل لبنان قريبا.
sameera: li'anni musaafira 'ilaa jabal lubnaan qareeban.
Samira: Because I'm traveling to Mount Lebanon soon.

أنيس: لاتنسي ثياب التزلّج.
'anees: laa tansi thiyaabut-tazalluj.
Anis: Don't forget your ski outfit.

■ To make singular nouns dual, add either ان or ين to the ending.

Example:

The masculine noun كتاب becomes كتابان or كتابين.

The feminine noun غرفة becomes غرفتان or غرفتين. The *taa' marbooTa* (ة) at the ending of feminine nouns changes into a regular *taa* ت before a suffix.

A Match the Arabic words and expressions with their English equivalent.

A. handkerchief   tannoora تنورة ـــــــ .1

B. jacket   sayr سير ـــــــ .2

C. coat   bantaloon بنطلون ـــــــ .3

D. tie   rabTat ʿunq ربطة عنق ـــــــ .4

E. skirt   kufoof كفوف ـــــــ .5

F. belt   mandeel منديل ـــــــ .6

G. pants   thawbul Hammaam ثوب الحمّام ـــــــ .7

H. shoes   miʿTaf معطف ـــــــ .8

I. gloves   Hidhaa' حذاء ـــــــ .9

J. bathrobe   sitra سترة ـــــــ .10

K. baseball cap   mayyo ميّو ـــــــ .11

L. bathing suit   qubbaʿat baysbool قبعة بيسبول ـــــــ .12

B In Arabic, what do you wear...?

1. ...to school?

_____

2. ...to a symphony concert?

_____

3. ...to bed?

_____

4. ...in cool weather?

_____

5. ...in cold weather?

_____

6. ...to a swimming pool?

_____

C
Complete the analogies.

1. كفوف: يدان
   kufoof: yadaan
   =
   = أقدام: _____
   'aqdaam: ....

2. _____ :تنورة
   tannoora: ....
   =
   = قميص: بنطلون
   qameeS: banTaloon

3. ثوب النوم: بيجاما
   beejaama: thawbun-nawm
   =
   = معطف: _____
   miʿTaf: ....

4. ربطة عنق: قميص
   qameeS: rabTat ʿunq
   =
   = بنطلون: _____
   banTaloon: ....

D
Complete each sentence with Arabic words that describe the pictures.

1. أنا ألبس _____.
   'anaa 'albus....

2. أنا ألبس _____.
   'anaa 'albus....

3. أنا ألبس _____.
   'anaa 'albus....

4. أنا ألبس _____
'anaa 'albus...

و _____.
wa...

5. أنا ألبس _____
'anaa 'albus...

و _____.
wa...

 Write the words or expressions in English.

1. اللبس allabs _____

2. يلبس / تلبس yalbus / talbus _____

3. ألبس 'albus _____

4. أنتَ (m.) تلبس 'anta talbus _____

5. أنتِ (f.) تلبسين 'anty talbiseen _____

F Fill in the blanks with examples in Arabic of the appropriate clothing according to the heading.

outdoor clothing

1. _____
2. _____
3. _____
4. _____

accessories

5. _____
6. _____
7. _____

footwear

8. _____
9. _____
10. _____

sleepwear

11. _____

G Choose the most logical answer to complete each sentence.

١. أجهّز...
'ujahhiz....

أ. حقيبتي Haqeebati

ب. مدينتي madeenati

ج. حديقتي Hadeeqati

د. إجازتي 'ijaazati

٢. أنت تلبس....
'anta talbus....

أ. حقيبة Haqeeba

ب. صحة SiHHa

ج. صف Saff

د. بنطلون وقميص banTaloon waqameeS

٣. تذكّر أن تأخذ....
tadhakkar 'an ta'khudh....

أ. الحديقة alHadeeqa

ب. الكفوف alkufoof

ج. جبل لبنان jabal lubnaan

د. بيروت bayroot

٤. أبحث على سترة لأني....
abHath ʿalaa sitra li'anni....

أ. انتظرني antaDHurni

ب. سترتي sitrati

ج. سأخرج إلى الحديقة sa'akhruj ilal-Hadeeqa

د. ألبس جاكيت 'albus jaakeet

٥. ألبس بذلة جديدة لأني....
'albus badhla jadeeda li'anni....

أ. مسافرا إلى جبل لبنان
mausaafiran 'ila jabal lubnaan

ب. عندي ربطة عنق جديدة
ʿindi rabTat ʿunq jadeeda

ج. ذاهب إلى الحفلة الموسيقيّة الليلة
dhaahib 'ilal-Haflal-mooseeqiyyal-layla

د. أجهّز حقيبتي 'ujahhiz Haqeebati

٦. المعطف....
almiʿTaf....

أ. قبعة بيسبول qubaʿat baysbool

ب. تنورة tannoora

ج. الليلة allayla

د. جميل jameel

H **Read the paragraph; then select the correct answers.**

سميرة (f.) ذاهبة في إجازة مع أسرتها. هي مسافرة إلى بيروت عاصمة لبنان.

sameera dhaahiba fi 'ijaaza maᶜ 'usratiha. hiya musaafira 'ila bayroot ᶜaaSimat lubnaan.

هي تجهّز حقيبتها. سميرة تجلب معها ملابس شتوية. تجلب معها

hiya tujahhiz Haqeebataha. sameera tajlub maᶜaha malaabis shatawiyya. tajlub maᶜaha

فقط: بنطلونان، كنزتان، فستان، تنورة، بلوزة وجاكيت.

faqaT: banTaloonan, kanzataan, fustaan, tannoora, blooza, wajaakeet.

كل الملابس الملائمة لرحلتها إلى لبنان معها.

kulul-malaabisil-mulaa'ima liriHlatiha ila lubnaan maᶜaha.

is going on vacation	**dhaahiba fee ijaaza**	ذاهبة في إجازة
She is packing her suitcase.	**tujahhiz Haqeebataha**	تجهّز حقيبتها
She is only bringing with her	**tajlub maᶜaha faqaT**	تجلب معها فقط
appropriate	**mula'aima**	ملائمة
all	**kull**	كل

٣. كم بنطلونا سميرة جالبة معها؟
kamm banTaloonan sameera jaaliba maᶜaha?

أ. أربعة 'arbaᶜa
ب. ثلاثة thalaatha
ج. إثنان 'ithnaan
د. واحد waaHid

١. من ذاهب في إجازة؟
mann dhaahib fee 'ijaaza?

أ. إجازة 'ijaaza
ب. بيروت bayroot
ج. لبنان lubnaan
د. سميرة sameera

٤. هل سميرة تجلب معها فستانا في حقيبتها؟
hal sameera tajlub maᶜaha fustaanan fee Haqeebatiha?

أ. نعم ، معها فستان واحد. naᶜam, maᶜaha fustaan waaHid.
ب. لا ، معها فستانان. laa, maᶜaha fustaanaan.
ج. لا ، معها ثلاثة فساتين. laa, maᶜaha thalaathat fasaateen.
د. لا ، لم تجلب معها فستان. laa, lam tajlub maᶜaha fustaan.

٢. ماذا تضع في حقيبتها؟
madha taDaᶜ fee Haqeebatiha?

أ. لبنان lubnaan
ب. أسرتها 'usratuha
ج. سميرة sameera
د. ملابس شتوية malaabis shatawiyya

I **In your opinion, what other articles of clothing should Samira take along for the cold winter days of February in Lebanon? Make a list in Arabic.**

_____

_____

_____

_____

_____

J لنتكلّم! (*linatakallam!*) Ask your speaking partner what he or she is wearing today: ماذا تلبس اليوم؟ (*maadha talbis alyawm?*) He / she should answer with: ألبس..... (*'albus....*) and then name several articles of clothing. Then reverse roles.

K دورك! (*dawrak!*) Your partner will choose a category of clothing, such as casual clothes, outdoor cold weather clothes, bedtime clothes, accessories, and clothes for special occasions. If you can correctly name all the items in that category in 20 seconds, give yourself a gold star. If you can't, or if the clock beats you, your partner takes over. This time, you select a category, and he / she will answer. Continue until all the categories are covered. The person with the most gold stars wins.

Proverb

" كل كما تريد والبس كما يريد الناس.
kul kama tureed walbis kama yureedun-naas.
Eat to please yourself and dress to please others. **"**

How Do I Write the Arabic Alphabet?

meem م and *noon* ن in the four different positions

Final	Medial	Initial	Independent
مـ	ـمـ	مـ	م
قلم	تمر	موز	ثوم
Writing Practice			
مـ	ـمـ	مـ	م
قلم	تمر	موز	ثوم

Final	Medial	Initial	Independent
ـن	ـنـ	نـ	ن
لبن	غني	نمل	لون
Writing Practice			
ـن	ـنـ	نـ	ن
لبن	غني	نمل	لون

Symtalk

L In the space, write the correct word or expression in Arabic.

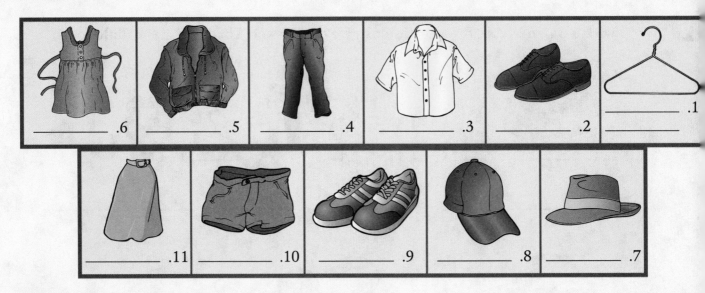

M Say the sentences, then write them in Arabic.

.5

Work with a partner. Ask the question or give the answer. Then, write the dialogue.

_____

.1

_____

_____

_____

.2

_____

_____

_____

.3

_____

_____

_____

.4

_____

_____

Living Language لغتنا الحيّة

lughatunal-Hayya

O **Look at the clippings to find the information requested below.**

1. A. The clipping with the arrows advertises "retail" and "wholesale" clothing. Circle these
   two words and then write them below.

   _____

   _____

   B. The clipping with the heading "Discovery Shopping Center" has reduced prices by 60%
   during their sale. In which month is the sale taking place?

   _____

2. Circle the letters ن and م on the clippings and write them below in the four positions:

Final	Medial	Initial	Independent

Unit 13

الوقت والألوان

alwaqt wal'alwaan

Time and Colors

169

كم الساعة؟
kam assaaᶜa?
What time is it?

الساعة الواحدة والنصف
assaaᶜatul-waaHida wanniSf

الساعة الثالثة
assaaᶜatuth-thaalitha

الساعة العاشرة إلا ربع
assaaᶜatul-ᶜaashira 'illa rubᶜ

ظهرا
DHuhran

في أي ساعة...؟
fee 'ayy saaᶜa...?
At what time...?

في الساعة الثانية وخمس دقائق
fis-saaᶜatith-thaaniya wakhams daqaa'iq

في الساعة السابعة والربع
fis-saaᶜatis-saabiᶜa warrubᶜ

في الساعة الحادية عشرة وخمسة وخمسين دقيقة
fis-saaᶜatil-Haadiya ᶜashra wakhamsat wakhamseen daqeeqa

في منتصف الليل
fee muntaSafil-layl

- Time in formal Arabic is stated by using ordinal numbers rather than cardinal numbers. For example, it's the "first" hour, the "second hour," the "tenth" hour, etc. See p.172 for a list of ordinal numbers.

- Time in formal Arabic is further described with صباحا (*SabaaHan*), morning; ظهرا (*DHuhran*), noon; مساءً (*masaa'an*), evening; or ليلًا (*laylan*), night.

ما لون...؟
maa lawn...?
What color is...?

ما ألوان...؟
maa 'alwaan...?
What color(s) are...?

هو....
huwa....
It is....

هي....
hiya....
They are....

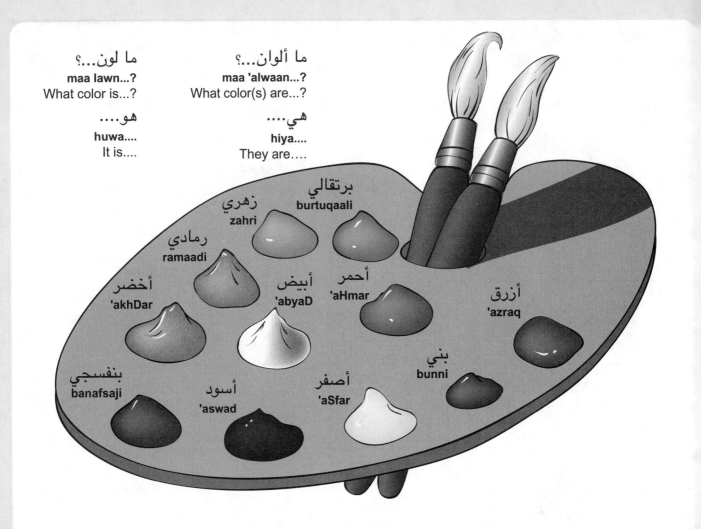

Category I				Category II			
Masculine		**Feminine**		**Masculine**		**Feminine**	
	أسود 'aswad		سوداء sawdaa'		بني bunni		بنيّة bunniyya
	أحمر 'aHmar		حمراء Hamraa'		برتقالي burtuqaali		برتقالية burtuqaaliyya
	أخضر 'akhDar		خضراء khaDraa'		زهري zahri		زهرية zahriyya
	أبيض 'abiaD		بيضاء bayDaa'		رمادي ramaadi		رمادية ramaadiyya
	أصفر 'aSfar		صفراء Safraa'		بنفسجي banafsaji		بنفسجية banafsajiyya
	أزرق 'azraq		Blue زرقاء zarqaa'		ذهبي dhahabi		Gold ذهبية dhahabiyya
					فضي fiDDi		Silver فضية fiDDiyya

Extra Vocabulary مفردات إضافيّة
mufradaat iDaafiyya

ثانية / ثواني **thaaniya / thawaany** second / seconds	دقيقة / دقائق **daqeeqa / daqaa'iq** minute / minutes	وقت / أوقات **waqt / awqaat** time / times

Ordinal numbers		Cardinal numbers	
	أوّل awwal		واحد waaHid
	ثاني thaany		إثنان ithnaan
	ثالث thaalith		ثلاثة thalaatha
	رابع raabiᶜ		أربعة arbaᶜa
	خامس khaamis		خمسة khamsa
	سادس saadis		ستة sitta
	سابع saabiᶜ		سبعة sabᶜa
	ثامن thaamin		ثمانية thamaaniya
	تاسع taasiᶜ		تسعة tisᶜa
	عاشر ᶜaashir		عشرة ᶜashara
	الحادية عشر alHaadiya ᶜashar		إحدى عشر iHda ᶜashar
	الثانية عشر aththaaniya ᶜashar		إثنا عشر ithna ᶜashar

A Listen as your teacher gives the time on one of the pictured clocks. Place an "A" to the left of that clock. Continue lettering until the time on all eight clocks has been given.

_____ .5

_____ .1

_____ .6

_____ .2

_____ .7

_____ .3

_____ .8

_____ .4

B **Complete the sentences with a color in Arabic. Use the masculine form of the color.**

1. Light red is called _____.

2. A bluebird or robin's egg is _____.

3. Chocolate is _____.

4. Lemons and dandelions are _____.

5. In the summer, a leaf is _____.

6. Tar is _____.

7. The color _____ is the same as the name of a fruit.

8. The sky on a very cloudy day looks _____.

9. A marshmallow is _____.

10. A strawberry is _____.

C **Write in Arabic.**

1. at seven o'clock _____

2. It's half past one. _____

3. at 8:10 _____

4. It's 2:40. _____

5. at twenty past three _____

D **What colors are they? Match the items in column A with their color in column B.**

B   A

أصفر A.
'aSfar

_____ .1

B. رمادي
ramaadi

_____ .2

C. أزرق
'azraq

_____ .3

D. أحمر
'aHmar

_____ .4

E. أخضر
'akhDar

_____ .5

E Answer with "yes" نعم (na‘am) or "no" لا (laa).

1. هل الحشيش أخضر؟
   halil-Hasheesh 'akhDar?   _____

2. هل البندورة زرقاء؟
   halil-banadoora zarqaa'?   _____

3. هل الفيل أصفر؟
   halil-feel 'aSfar?   _____

4. هل الموز برتقالي؟
   halil-mawz burtuqaali?   _____

5. هل الفراولة حمراء؟
   halil-faraawila Hamraa'?   _____

F Read the paragraph, then circle the correct answers.

باسم (m.) سيذهب إلى السينما مع صديقته ندين (f.). الفيلم يبدأ في الساعة
baasim sayadhhab 'ilas-seenama ma‘ Sadeeqatihi nadeen. alfeelm yabda' fis-saa‘atith

الثامنة مساءً. باسم سيلبس قميصاً أبيضاً وربطة عنق حمراء.
thaamina masaa'an. baasim sayalbus qameeSan 'abyaDan warabTat ‘unq Hamraa'.

ندين ستلبس بلوزتها الصفراء وكلساتها الصفراء وتنورتها الخضراء.
nadeen satalbus bloozatahaS-Safraa' wakalsaatahaS-Safraa' watanooratahal-khaDraa'.

الاثنان يلبسان أحذية سوداء. الساعة الآن السابعة والربع. باسم يذهب
alithnaan yalbisaan 'aHdhiya sawdaa'. assaa‘atul-'aan assaabi‘a warrub‘. baasim yadhhab

إلى بيت ندين.
'ila bayt nadeen

the film starts	الفيلم يبدأ **alfeelm yabda'**	will go	سيذهب **sayadhhab**
is going to wear (m.)	سيلبس **sayalbus**	to the movie theater	إلى السينما **'ilas-seenama**
is going to wear (f.)	ستلبس **satalbus**	his friend	صديقته **Sadeeqatuhu**

1. من صديق باسم؟
   mann Sadeeq baasim?

أ. والدته walidatuhu

ب. جاد jaad

ج. أخته 'ukhtuhu

هـ. ندين nadeen

2. باسم وندين يذهبان....
   baasim wanadeen yadhhabaan....

أ. إلى الريف 'ilar-reef

ب. إلى المطعم 'ilal-maT‘am

ج. إلى السينما 'ilas-seenama

هـ. إلى المنتزه 'ilal-muntazah

5. في أي ساعة باسم سيذهب إلى بيت ندين؟
fee ayy saaʿa baasim sayadhhab 'ila bayt nadeen?

أ. في السابعة والربع
fis-saabiʿa warrubʿ

ب. في السابعة إلا ربع
fis-saabiʿa 'illa rubʿ

ج. في السادسة والنصف
fis-saadisa wanniSf

هـ. في الثامنة
fith-thaamina

6. في أي ساعة يبدأ الفيلم؟
fee 'ayy saaʿa yabda'ul-feelm?

أ. السابعة
assaabiʿa

ب. السابعة والربع
assaabiʿa warrubʿ

ج. الثامنة
aththaamina

هـ. الثامنة والنصف
aththaamina wanniSf

3. ما لون ربطة عنق باسم؟
maa lawn rabTat ʿunq baasim?

أ. خضراء
khaDraa'

ب. حمراء
Hamraa'

ج. زرقاء
zarqaa'

هـ. بيضاء
bayDaa'

4. ما لون كلسات ندين؟
maa lawn kalsaat nadeen?

أ. صفراء
Safraa'

ب. بنية
bunniyya

ج. سوداء
sawdaa'

هـ. رمادية
ramaadiyya

G **Color the clock according to the directions that follow on the next page.**

7. رقم أربعة: أسود
raqam 'araba'a: aswad

8. رقم ستة: بنفسجي
raqam sitta: banafsaji

9. رقم ثلاثة: أحمر
raqam thalaatha: 'aHmar

10. رقم اثنا عشر: أبيض
raqam ithnaa 'ashar: 'abyaD

11. رقم عشرة: زهري
raqam 'ashara: zahri

12. رقم خمسة: أسود
raqam khamsa: 'aswad

1. الأنف: أصفر
al'anf: 'aSfar

2. العيون: زرقاء
al'uyoon: zarqaa'

3. الشعر: أخضر
ashsha'r: 'akhDar

4. الوجه: برتقالي
alwajh: burtuqaali

5. الفم: بني
alfamm: bunni

6. الأقدام: رمادية
al'aqdaam: ramaadiyya

H لنتكلّم! (*linatakallam!*) You want to know at what time certain things take place, for example, math class, the concert, the picnic. Start with في أي وقت؟ (*fee ayy waqt?*). Your partner should answer you by mentioning a specific time of day or evening.

I لنتكلّم! (*linatakallam!*) Your speaking partner will give you six times of day in Arabic. For each, answer with the correct greeting: Good morning: صباح الخير (*SabaaHul khayr*) or Good evening: مساء الخير (*masaa'ul khayr*). When you finish, reverse roles.

J دورك! (*dawrak!*) Select a quizmaster from the students in your class. He or she will walk around the classroom and point to certain objects and ask: ما لون هذا؟ (*maa lawn haadha?*) A classmate will answer: هو/هي (*huwa / hiya*), naming the correct color. If someone answers incorrectly, he / she drops out of the contest. The quizmaster keeps going, pointing to different objects, until there is just one classmate left. That person is the winner.

Proverb

لاحقا خير من أبدا!
laaHiqan khayrun min 'abadan!
Better late than never!

How Do I Write the Arabic Alphabet?

haa ‫هـ‬ and *waaw* ‫و‬ in the four different positions

Final	Medial	Initial	Independent
‫ـه‬	‫ـهـ‬	‫هـ‬	‫ه‬
‫بليه‬	‫مهر‬	‫هدهد‬	‫مياه‬
Writing Practice			

Final	Medial	Initial	Independent
‫ـو‬	‫ـو‬	‫و‬	‫و‬
‫حلو‬	‫موز‬	‫وتر‬	‫جرو‬
Writing Practice			

Symtalk

K

On the blanks, write the masculine and feminine forms of the colors in Arabic.

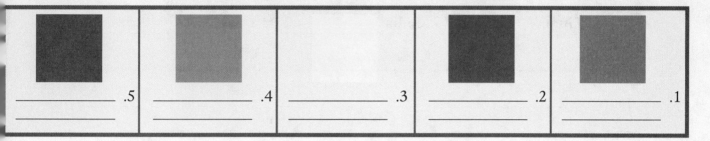

_____ .5	_____ .4	_____ .3	_____ .2	_____ .1
_____	_____	_____	_____	_____

L

Say the sentences, then write them in Arabic.

.1

_____

.2

_____

.3

_____

.4

_____

.5

_____

١.

٢.

٣.

٤.

٥.

Living Language لغتنا الحيّة

lughatunal-Hayya

👑

رولكس

ساعة رولكس ليدي - ديت جَست مــن الذهب الأصفر عيار ١٨ قيراطاً . الاطار مرصـع بـ٣٢ ألماسة (١,٤٥ قـيـراط تقريباً) ، أما السوار فهو مرصَع بـ ١٧٤ ألماسة صغيرة (٢,٣٥ قيراط تقريباً) و١٤ زمردة (٣,٤٢ قيراط تقريباً) . إن روعـة هـذا الـطـراز يـتـجـلـى بـالمـيـنـا المصنوعة من الحجر الكريم ذو اللون الأخضر الضارب إلى السواد والمرصّعة بـ ١٠ ألماسات.

الخاتم مصنـوع مـن الذهب الأصفـر عيـار ١٨ قيراطاً و٢٦ مـاسـة صغيرة (٠,٥٢ قيراط تقريباً) تـزيـده تـألقاً ألماسة كبيرة (٠,٢٢ قيراط تقريباً).

N **Look at the clipping to find the information requested below.**

1. A. What is the brand name of the advertised watch?

   _____

   B. What is the time shown on the watch?

   _____

2. Circle the letters ي ، و ، and هـ in the clippings and write them below in the four positions:

Final	Medial	Initial	Independent

Unit 14

الموسيقى

almooseeqa

Music

عود
ᶜuood
lute

ألحان
'alHaan
melodies

مغنّية
mughanniya
female singer

مغنّي
mughanny
male singer

طبلة
Tabla
single drum

ناي
naay
flute

حفلة
Hafla
party

مسرح
masraH
theater

دفّ
daff
tambourine

بيانو
biaano
piano

قانون
qaanoon
zither

كمان
kamaan
violin

Dialogues

سامي (m.): هل تريدين الذهاب إلى المسرح؟
saamy: hal tureedeena dh-dhahab 'ilal-masraH?
Sami: Do you want to go to the theatre?

سامية (f.): نعم ، أحب فيروز كثيرا.
saamia: na'am, 'uHibbu fayrooz katheeran.
Samia: Yes, I like Faiyruz a lot.

سمير (m.): هل تحبين هذه الأغنية؟
sameer: hal tuHibeen hadhihil-'ughniya?
Samir: Do you like this song?

سميرة (f.): نعم ، أنا أحب المغنية نانسي عجرم كثيرا.
sameera: na'am, 'anaa 'uHibul-mughanniya naancy 'ajram katheeran.
Samira: Yes, I like the singer Nancy Ajram a lot.

باسم (m.): لماذا لا تأتي معنا إلى الحفلة؟
baasim: limaadha laa ta'ti ma'ana 'ilal-Hafla?
Basim: Why don't come with us to the party?

باسمة (f.): أنا مشغولة اليوم ، مروان يذهب معك.
baasima: 'anaa mashghoolal-yawm. marwaan yadhhab ma'ak.
Basima: I am busy today. Marwan can go with you.

نبيل (m.): هذا المساء سأستمع إلى البيانو والقانون.
nabeel: haadhal-masaa' sa'astami' 'ilal-biaano walqaanoon.
Nabil: This evening I will listen to the piano and the zither.

نبيلة (f.): أنا أفضّل العود والدف.
nabeela: 'anaa 'ufaDilul-'uood waddaf.
Nabila: I prefer the lute and the tambourine.

جميلة (f.): هل يمكنك أن تعزف على الكمان والناي والطبلة؟
jameela: hal umkinuka 'an ta'zuf 'alal-kamaan wannaay waTTabla?
Jamila: Are you able to play the violin, the flute, and the single drum?

جميل (m.): نعم، أنا أعزف على الكمان ولكن لا أحب الناي والطبلة.
jameel: na'am 'anaa 'a'zuf 'alal-kamaan walaakin laa 'uHibun-naay waTTabla.
Jamil: Yes, I play the violin, but I don't like the lute and the single drum.

Great Arab Musicians عظماء الموسيقى العربية
ᶜuDHamaa'ul-mooseeqal-ᶜarabiyya

muHammad ᶜabdul-wahhab (1901–1991) is Egypt's best known composer, singer, and actor. He created a new genre in Arab music by introducing western instruments to Arab melodies. His new style of music dazzled the king, the notables, and the porters alike. As a Muslim, he began his career by reciting Qur'anic verses in the *madrasa*. He mastered the *ᶜuood* (lute), the most popular instrument in Arab music. *ᶜabdul-wahhab* managed to combine the oriental quarter note with Western half and full notes to create a unique ornamentation that set the stage for the modern song in Arabic. After Egypt became a republic in the early '50's, he produced his best work on stage and in musical films that were influenced by Hollywood. He composed one of the most famous musical compositions and Arabic songs. His composition of أنت عمري *'anta ᶜumri* for the legendary diva أم كلثوم *'umm kulthoom* is considered a historical masterpiece of voice and melody.

Mansur Rahbani's musical The Reign of the Shepherds

al'akhawayn raHbaani—Rahbani Brothers: (ᶜaaSee raHbaani 1923–1986, and manSoor raHbaani 1925–) are among the most celebrated Arab musicians of the 20th century. They began their musical career in affiliation with a choir in a church. They later studied music in Lebanon and managed to introduce a new theme in Arab songs unprecedented in Middle Eastern music. They combined the tunes of the lute, the piano, and the violin to create a unique and distinctive blend of melodies. They revived an old musical style known as موشحات *muwashshaHaat* and adapted western compositions in a new Middle Eastern approach and technique. They composed scores of original short songs, which attracted the most notable musicians in the country to work with them in the '50's and in later decades. Their hard work subsequently gave rise to a new genre of Lebanese musicals, which continued on the stages of Baalbeck, the internationally acclaimed festival, until the outbreak of the Lebanese Civil War in the mid '70's. In their musicals, فيروز *fayrooz*, the wife of ᶜaaSee and a notable icon of Arab performers, sang their melodies and new compositions in a voice that amazed and astounded Arab audiences. The *raHbaani* did in fact reinvent Arabic music in a modern and innovative style. They compared rural and urban life, traditions and modernity, and most of all love of and faith in the motherland.

fareedal-'aTrash (1915–1974), born in Southern Syria near the town of Swaida to a notable Druze family, moved to Egypt with his family when he was in his teens. It was in القاهرة (Cairo) that *fareed* launched his music career. He became interested in music along with his sister *asmahaan,* who also became a famous star. *alaTrash* worked with the famous composers of the time, including رياض السنباطي (*riyaaD aSSunbaaTi*). He later presented his own compositions to create a new *maqaam* of *ʿuood* (lute) ornamentations. He sang to his own tunes and became an actor introducing new compositions with each new film he starred in. His musical films, like the *ʿabdul-wahhab* films, were somewhat influenced by Hollywood productions. People in the Arab world impatiently waited for his new films to open. He heralded in a new culture of music, songs, and dance. *fareed* was also one of the most famous Arab percussionists of the 20th century.

Nancy Ajram

Popular Music

Music in the Arab world has recently reached new heights. The rise of satellite stations and increased interactions between Arab people and the rest of the world have influenced the culture of music. The most popular media element today is the video clip. Arab singers and performers are keen on presenting their work in short video segments, which reflect the essence of the song or the message it espouses. In addition, a number of performers are combining English, French, and Spanish with Arabic. Some of the new tunes are incredibly unique to the world of music. The new generation of popular Arab singers includes but is not limited to the following:

From Lebanon:

naancy ʿajram (*f.*) نانسي عجرم
najwa karam (*f.*) نجوى كرم
ʿaaSil-Hallaani (*m.*) عاصي الحلاني
aleessa (*f.*) اليسا
raamil-ʿayyash (*m.*) رامي العياش
waa'il kafoori (*m.*) وائل كفوري

Nawal

Ahlam

From Syria:
'asaala (*f.*) أصالة
george wassouf (*m.*) جورج وصوف

From Tunisia:
Sabirir-rubaaᶜi (*m.*) صابر الرباعي
laTeefa (*f.*) لطيفة

From Algeria:
fulla (*f.*) فلة

From Egypt:
ᶜamr dhiaab (*m.*) عمرو ذياب
'anghaam (*f.*) أنغام
hishaam ᶜabbaas (*m.*) هشام عباس
ehaab tawfeeq (*m.*) أيهاب توفيق
shereen (*f.*) شيرين

From Iraq:
kaaDHimas-saahir (*m.*) كاظم الساهر

From Kuwait:
ᶜabdalla ruwayshid (*m.*) عبدالله رويشد
nabeel shaᶜayl (*m.*) نبيل شعيل
nawaal (*f.*) نوال

From Saudi Arabia:
ᶜabdul-majeed ᶜabdalla (*m.*) عبد المجيد عبدالله

From United Arab Emirates:
ᶜabdallah bilkhayr (*m.*) عبدالله بلخير
'aHlaam (*f.*) أحلام

From Yemen:
'aHmad fatHi (*m.*) أحمد فتحي

From Sudan:
rashaa (*f.*) رشا

From Morocco:
Hasnaa (*f.*) حسنا

From Libya:
(*m.*) حميد الشاعري
Hameedash-shaaᶜree

Dance

Popular performers in recent years have enhanced their music productions with multiple forms of dance. Some have been adaptations to already established western dance and some a reinvention of traditional dances. Other forms of dance include a combination of both eastern and western forms. The two basic forms of Arab dance include the Belly Dance and *Dabka*. The former is performed solo with variations of hand and leg movements accompanied by extreme flexibility in body swaying. In social events, however, a group of partners may be seen dancing together. The latter dance is a group dance. Dancers normally hold hands, shoulder to shoulder, in a straight line, or in a circular formation. *Dabka* is performed with rapid and simultanous movement of feet, legs, and / or shoulders. The dance varies in form and style from one region to the other and is more popular in rural areas where people are more community oriented.

Palestinians dancing the Dabka

Activities نشاطات

nashaaTaat

A **Give the full name of the composer who...**

1. . . . launched a series of musicals in the '60's and early '70's.
   _____

2. . . . started singing in the *madrasa*.
   _____

3. . . . moved to Egypt and composed and sang his tunes in films.
   _____

B **Write an أ to identify string instruments and a ب to identify non-string instruments.**

_____ عود .1
uood‘

_____ طبلة .2
Tabla

_____ كمان .3
kamaan

_____ قانون .4
qaanoon

_____ ناي .5
naay

_____ دفّ .6
daff

C **Identify. . .**

1. . . . the name of the singer who sang the *raHbaani* Brothers' musicals.
   _____

2. . . . where *fareedal-'aTrash* established his musical career.
   _____

3. . . . the names of two female Lebanese singers.
   _____

4. . . . the name of the composer who wrote *anta ‘umri*.
   _____

5. . . . the name of two Egyptian male vocalists.
   _____

Unit 14　　　almooseeqa الموسيقى　　　**190**

6. . . . the name of the dance that is performed in groups.

_____

7. . . . the name of the old musical style revived by the *raHbaani* Brothers.

_____

8. . . . which instrument was used by *fareedal-'aTrash*.

_____

9. . . . a style of dance performed solo.

_____

10. . . . the composer who combined the oriental quarter and western half note.

_____

D **Match the illustrations with the names.**

A. عود
'uood

_____ .1

B. طبلة
Tabla

_____ .2

C. كمان
kamaan

_____ .3

D. قانون
qaanoon

_____ .4

E. ناي
naay

_____ .5

E دورك! *(dawrak!)* **Choose one of the following singers, musicians, or composers. Do a brief search on your computer search engine to find out as much as you can about the person's life and music. Report your findings to the class using as many Arabic words as you can. A musical excerpt on an audio CD would add a nice touch to your presentation.**

أنغام (*f.*) 'anghaam

هشام عباس (*m.*) hishaam 'abbaas

أيهاب توفيق (*m.*) ehaab tawfeeq

شيرين (*f.*) shereen

كاظم الساهر (*m.*) kaaDHimas-saahir

عبدالله رويشد (*m.*) ᶜabdalla ruwayshid

نبيل شعيل (*m.*) nabeel shaᶜayl

نانسي عجرم (*f.*) naancy ᶜajram

نجوى كرم (*f.*) najwa karam

عاصي الحلاني (*m.*) ᶜaaSil-Hallaani

اليسا (*f.*) aleessa

صابر الرباعي (*m.*) Sabirir-rubaaᶜi

لطيفة (*f.*) laTeefa

فلة (*f.*) fulla

عمرو ذياب (*m.*) ᶜamr dhiaab

Shirin

Proverb

" الموسيقى تنعش القلوب وتبعد الذنوب.
**almooseeqa tunᶜishul-quloob
watubᶜidudh-dhunoob.**
Music makes the heart grow light
and makes trouble go away. "

How Do I Write the Arabic Alphabet?

yaa ي in the four different positions. Other characters used in writing: *kursy yaa* ئ

Final	Medial	Initial	Independent
ي	ـيـ	يـ	ي
صبي	بيت	يد	شاي
Writing Practice			
ــيّ	ــيبيـ	ايبيـ	يّ
ـصـبيـن	بيبيبـت	ـيبـ	ـثـشاي

Final	Medial	Initial	Independent
ـئ	ـئـ		ئ
شاطئ	طائرة		طوارئ
Writing Practice			
ـئ	ـئـ		ئ
ـثـشـاطـئ	طـائـرة		طـوارئ

Symtalk

F In the spaces, write the correct words in Arabic.

G Say the sentences, then write them in Arabic.

 ٥.

H **Work with a partner. Ask the question or give the answer. Then, write the dialogue.**

   إلى ١.

_____
_____

   إلى ٢.

_____
_____

   و و إلى ٣.

_____
_____

    إلى ٤.

_____
_____

يفخــر Café Rio برمانـا ان يقدم

ســلطان الطــرب

جـــورج وســـوف

نجم استديو الفــن   مـــلاك لبنان

مروان حاطــوم   ليليــانا صالحــة

يقدم البرنامج مونولوجيست لبنـان : زكور

الجمعـــة ٢٠ آب ١٩٩٣

على ملعب مدرسة مار انطونيوس ـ حمانا الساعة الثامنة والنصف مساء

سعر البطاقة ١٥ $

№   169

رامي عياش
في
سهرة فنية استثنائية مميزة
٩:٣٠ مساء السبت ٢٣ تموز ٢٠٠٥
ملعب المدرسة الرسمية ـ رأس المتن

I

Look at the clippings to find the information requested below.

1. A. At what time does the music party at Café Rio start?

   _____

   B. The clipping of the man with glasses mentions a concert. At what time does the concert start?

   _____

2. A. In the clipping that has the number "169," find the Arabic word for "schedule."

   _____

   B. In the same clipping you will find some names in Arabic. Write any two of the names.

   _____

   _____

Unit 15

الطقس والفصول

aTTaqs walfuSool

Weather and Seasons

Vocabulary المفردات
almufradaat

| How's the weather? | **kayfaT-Taqs / aljaww?** | كيف الطقس/ الجو؟ |

الطقس معتدل.
aTTaqs muᶜtadil.
The weather is moderate.

الطقس جميل.
aTTaqs jameel.
The weather is nice.

مشمس.	حار.	بارد.	عاصف.	مرطب.	غائم.
mushmis.	**Haar.**	**baarid.**	**ᶜaaSif.**	**murTib.**	**ghaa'im.**
It's sunny.	It's warm (hot).	It's cool.	It's windy.	It's humid.	It's cloudy.

The weather is bad. **aTTaqs ᶜaaTil.** الطقس عاطل.

راعد.	ممطر.	بارق.	بارد.	مثلج.
raaᶜid.	**mumTir.**	**baariq.**	**baarid.**	**muthlij.**
It's thundering.	It's raining.	It's lightning.	It's cold.	It's snowing.

أي فصل هذا؟
'ayy faSl haadha?
What season is this?

هـو....
huwa....
It's....

The four seasons alfuSoolul-'arba^ca الفصول الأربعة

summer **Sayf** صيف

spring **rabee^c** ربيع

winter **shitaa'** شتاء

autumn / fall **khareef** خريف

■ In the summer (same pattern for the other seasons) = **fiS-Sayf** في الصيف

■ Notice the verb forms based on nouns.

thunder	=	**ra^cd**	رعد	→	It's thundering.	=	**tar^cud**	ترعد
lightning	=	**barq**	برق	→	It's lightning.	=	**tabruq**	تبرق
rain	=	**maTar**	مطر	→	It's raining.	=	**tumTir**	تمطر
snow	=	**thalj**	ثلج	→	It's snowing.	=	**tuthlij**	تثلج

Mother: Take your umbrella. **al'umm: khudh miDHalatuka.** الأم: خذ مظلتك.
Boy: Why? **alwalad: limaadha?** الولد: لماذا؟
Mother: It's raining. **al'umm: li'annaha tumTir.** الأم: لأنها تمطر.

Father: Wear your hat. **al'ab: albisi qubba^catuki.** الأب: البسي قبعتك.
Girl: Why? **albint: limaadha?** البنت: لماذا؟

الأب: لأن الجو بارد في الخارج.
al'ab: li'annal-jaww baarid fil-khaarij.
Father: Because it's cold out.

الأم: البس نظارتك.
al'umm: 'ulbus naDHaaratuka.
Mother: Wear your sunglasses.

الولد: لماذا؟
alwalad: limaadha?
Boy: Why?

الأم: لأن الجو مشمس.
al'umm: li'annal-jaww mushmis.
Mother: Because the weather is sunny.

A **Match each picture with its description.**

A. مشمس mushmis

_____ .1

B. بارق baariq

_____ .2

C. ممطر mumTir

_____ .3

D. عاصف ʿaaSif

_____ .4

E. بارد baarid

_____ .5

B **How's the weather? Answer this question in Arabic according to each picture.**

_____ .1

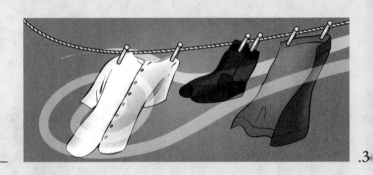

_____ .2

_____ .3

_____ .4

_____ .5

Match the picture with the season.

A. صيف Sayf

1. _____

B. شتاء 'shitaa

2. _____

C. ربيع ᶜrabee

3. _____

D. خريف khareef

4. _____

D Write in Column 1 the English meaning of each Arabic word. When you have finished the entire column, cover the column of Arabic words on the right. Then in Column 2, change the English words from Column 1 into Arabic.

Column 2 (Arabic)	Column 1 (English)	
_____	_____	1. شمس shams
_____	_____	2. برق barq
_____	_____	3. ربيع rabeeᶜ
_____	_____	4. صيف Sayf
_____	_____	5. طقس Taqs
_____	_____	6. خريف khareef
_____	_____	7. فصل faSl
_____	_____	8. بارد baarid
_____	_____	9. حار Haar
_____	_____	10. ممطر mumTir
_____	_____	11. شتاء' shitaa'
_____	_____	12. عاطل ᶜaaTil
_____	_____	13. رعد raᶜd
_____	_____	14. برد bard

E Match the nouns on the right with the related verbs on the left.

A. مشمس mushmis	1. _____ مطر maTar
B. ترعد tarᶜud	2. _____ ثلج thalj
C. تبرق tabruq	3. _____ رعد raᶜd
D. تثلّج tuthlij	4. _____ برق barq
E. تمطر tumTir	5. _____ شمس shams

F كيف الطقس؟ *(kayfaT-Taqs?)* **Use the cues to write a sentence in Arabic about the weather.**

1. mittens and parka

   _____

2. sunglasses

   _____

3. lightning bolts

   _____

4. light sweater

   _____

5. outdoor tennis court

   _____

6. umbrella

   _____

7. snowflakes

   _____

8. air conditioner

   _____

9. sailboat

   _____

10. rain, wind, and hail

    _____

G Read the paragraph; then circle the correct letter.

الفصول الأربعة
alfuSoolul-'arba⁵a
The Four Seasons

في الشتاء الطقس بارد جدا. تثلج كثيرا. الثلج أبيض. في الربيع الجو بارد
fish-shitaa' aTTaqs baarid jiddan. tuthlij katheeran. aththalj 'abyaD. fir-rabee⁵
aljaww baarid

وتمطر احيانا. الطقس حار ومشمس جدا في الصيف. في الخريف الجو عاصف
watumTir aHyaanan. aTTaqs Haar wamushmis jiddan fiS-Sayf. fil-khareef aljaww ⁵aaSif

وبارد أيضا. الفصول الأربعة مشوقة جدا.
wabaarid 'ayDan. alfuSoolul-'arba⁵a mushawwiqa jiddan.

---

sometime **aHyaanan** أحيانا		very **jiddan** جدا	
there is / there are **hunaaka** هناك		as well / also **ayDan** أيضا	

---

3. الجو حار جدا _____ .
aljaww Haar jiddan....

أ. في الشتاء fish-shitaa'

ب. في الخريف fil-khareef

ج. في الربيع fir-rabee⁵

د. في الصيف fiS-Sayf

1. فصل الشتاء _____ في مينيسوتا.
faSlush-shitaa'... fee menesoota.

أ. بارد baarid

ب. حار Haar

ج. عاصف ⁵aaSif

د. مشمس جدا mushmis jiddan

---

4. هناك _____ فصول.
hunaak... fuSool.

أ. خمسة khamsa

ب. أربعة 'arba⁵a

ج. ستة sitta

د. ثلاثة thalaatha

2. تمطر كثيرا _____ .
tumTir katheeran....

أ. في الربيع fir-rabee⁵

ب. في الصيف fiS-Sayf

ج. في الشتاء fish-shitaa'

د. في الخريف fil-khareef

Weather and Seasons

H لنتكلّم! (*linatakallam!*) Think of three clothing items or accessories. For each one you select, ask your partner to say how the weather is. Then reverse your roles. Your partner will suggest to you three new cues that you can respond to.

مثال:
mithaal:
Example:

A. نظّارات شمسيّة naDHDHaaraat shamsiyya
كيف الطقس؟ kayfaT-Taqs?
B. مشمس. mushmis.

I دورك! (*dawrak!*) Select five cities in various parts of the world and five different months. Use cities in different continents and hemispheres. Ask your partner about the weather in one of those cities. Your partner then should respond appropriately according to the city and month. (Don't forget that when it's summer in the northern hemisphere, it is winter in the southern hemisphere!) Write your answers on a piece of paper.

مثال:
mithaal:
Example:

A. كيف يكون الطقس في طوكيو في يناير؟
kayfa yakoonuT-Taqs fee Tookiyo fee-yanaayir?
B. بارد
baarid

Proverb

اليوم الغائم تنيره ابتسامة.
alyawmul-ghaa'im tuneerahu ibtisaama.
A smile brightens a cloudy day.

How Do I Write the Arabic Alphabet?

kursy waaw وَ and *taa' marbooTa* ة

Final	Medial	Initial	Independent
ـؤ	ـؤ		ؤ
لؤلؤ	بؤرة		رؤوس
Writing Practice			
ـؤ	ـؤ		ؤ
لؤلؤ	بؤرة		رؤوس

Final	Medial	Initial	Independent
ـة			ة
جامعة			سيّارة
Writing Practice			
ـة			ة
جامعة			سيّارة

Symtalk

J In the space, write the correct expression in Arabic.

_____.5	_____.4	_____.3	_____.2	_____.1

K Say the sentences, then write them in Arabic.

.1

_____

.2

_____

.3

_____

.4

_____

.5

_____

L **Work with a partner. Ask the question or give the answer. Then, write the dialogue.**

هل	☀️	؟

.1 هل ... ؟

_____ ‎(laa) لا

_____

.2 هل ... ؟

_____ ‎(laa) لا

_____

.3 هل ... ؟

_____ نعم ‎(na°am)

_____

.4 هل ... ؟

_____ ‎(laa) لا

_____

.5 هل ... ؟

_____ ‎(laa) لا

_____

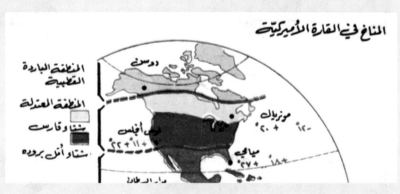

M **Look at the clippings to find the information requested below.**

1. Which two U.S. cities are mentioned on the map of the American continent?

   _____

   _____

2. Name the sport in Arabic that is pictured in the top clipping.

   _____

Unit 16

الأيام والشهور

al'ayyaam washshuhoor

Days and Months

مارس						
السبت	الجمعة	الخميس	الأربعاء	الثلاثاء	الاثنين	الأحد
٣	٢	١				
١٠	٩	٨	٧	٦	٥	٤
١٧	١٦	١٥	١٤	١٣	١٢	١١
٢٤	٢٣	٢٢	٢١	٢٠	١٩	١٨
٣١	٣٠	٢٩	٢٨	٢٧	٢٦	٢٥

ما اليوم؟		اليوم هو....
mal-yawm?		**alyawm huwa....**
What day is today?		Today is....

السبت **assabt** Saturday	الجمعة **aljum°a** Friday	الخميس **alkhamees** Thursday	الأربعاء **al'arbi°aa'** Wednesday	الثلاثاء **aththulaathaa'** Tuesday	الاثنين **al'ithnayn** Monday	الأحد **al'aHad** Sunday
7	6	5	4	3	2	1
14	13	12	11	10	9	8
21	20	19	18	17	16	15
28	27	26	25	24	23	22
				31	30	29

When is the holiday?	**mataal-'ijaaza?**	متى الإجازة؟
It's tomorrow.	**hiya ghadan.**	هي غدا.
What is the date today?	**maa huwa tareekhul-yawm?**	ما هو تاريخ اليوم؟
It's May 1st.	**'awwal 'ayyaar.**	أوّل أيار.
June 24	**'arba°a wa°ishreen Hazeeraan**	24 حزيران
September 15	**khamsata °ashar 'aylool**	15 أيلول

March **aathaar** آذار	September **'aylool** أيلول
April **neesaan** نيسان	October **tishreen 'awwal** تشرين أوّل
May **'ayyaar** أيار	November **tishreen thaani** تشرين ثاني
June **Hazeeraan** حزيران	December **kanoon 'awwal** كانون أوّل
July **tammooz** تمّوز	January **kanoon thaani** كانون ثاني
August **aab** آب	February **shubaaT** شباط

■ When you want to refer to the first day of any month, use the word for "first":
الأول من كانون ثاني **al'awwal min kanoon thaani.** الأول **al'awwal.**

■ When you write the date, be sure to put the day before the month.

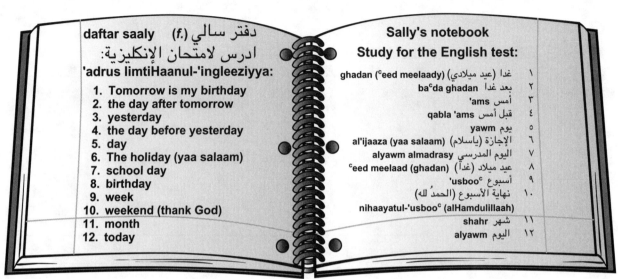

daftar saaly (f.) دفتر سالي

ادرس لامتحان الإنكليزية:

'adrus limtiHaanul-'ingleeziyya:

1. Tomorrow is my birthday
2. the day after tomorrow
3. yesterday
4. the day before yesterday
5. day
6. The holiday (yaa salaam)
7. school day
8. birthday
9. week
10. weekend (thank God)
11. month
12. today

Sally's notebook
Study for the English test:

١ غدا (عيد ميلادي) ghadan (ᶜeed meelaady)
٢ بعد غدا baᶜda ghadan
٣ أمس 'ams
٤ قبل أمس qabla 'ams
٥ يوم yawm
٦ الإجازة (ياسلام) al'ijaaza (yaa salaam)
٧ اليوم المدرسي alyawm almadrasy
٨ عيد ميلاد (غداً) ᶜeed meelaad (ghadan)
٩ أسبوع 'usbooᶜ
١٠ نهاية الأسبوع (الحمدُ لله) nihaayatul-'usbooᶜ (alHamdulillaah)
١١ شهر shahr
١٢ اليوم alyawm

رحاب (f.): ماذا تفعل اليوم يا رواد؟

riHaab: maadha tafᶜalul-yawm yaa rawaad?
Rihab: What do you have today, Rawad?

رواد (m.): لاشيء! راحة كل اليوم.

rawaad: laa shay'! raaHa kullal-yawm.
Rawad: Nothing! Today I've got a free day.

جوليات (f.): ماذا تفعل يوم الأربعاء؟

jooliyaat: madhaa tafᶜal yawmul-'arbiᶜaa'?
Juliet: What do you have on Wednesday?

سماح (f.): عندي درس كل اليوم.

samaaH: ᶜindee dars kullal-yawm.
Samah: I have to study all day.

سليم (m.): متى عيد ميلادك يا ملحم؟

saleem: mata ᶜeed meelaaduka yaa milHim?
Salim: When's your birthday, Milhim?

ملحم (m.): بعد غدا، الثامن من حزيران.

milHim: baᶜda ghadan, aththaamin min Hazeeran.
Milhim: It's the day after tomorrow, on June 8th.

رياض (m.): متى عندك امتحان الإنكليزية؟

riaaD: mata ᶜindak 'imtiHaanul-'ingleeziyya?
Riyad: What day do you have the English test?

زيد (m.): يوم الثلاثاء.

zayd: yawmuth-thulaathaa'.
Zayd: It's on Tuesday.

سلمان (m.): متى إجازة الربيع؟

salmaan: mata 'ijaazatur-rabeeᶜ?
Salman: When is spring break?

شادي (m.): بعد أسبوع واحد.

shaadi: baᶜda 'usbooᶜ waHid.
Shadi: In a week.

Activities نشاطات

nashaaTaat

A **Write in numerical form the dates that your teacher reads.**

> مثال :
> mithaal:
> *Example:*
>
> al'ustaadh yaqool: thalaatheen deesambar ٣٠ ديسمبر :الأستاذ يقول
> **Teacher says:**
>
> 'anta taktub: thalaatheen / 'ithna ᶜashar ٣٠ / ١٢ :أنت تكتب
> **You write:** *12/30*

_____ .4   _____ .1

_____ .5   _____ .2

                                       _____ .3

B **Label the current month. Include the names of the days and all the numbers.**

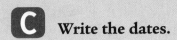 **Write the dates.**

مثال :
mithaal:
Example:
Tuesday, February 11ᵗʰ
الثلاثاء ١١ شباط
aththulaathaa' 'iHda ᶜashar shubaaT

1. Wednesday, October 22ⁿᵈ

   _____

2. Sunday, August 13ᵗʰ

   _____

3. Thursday, May 1ˢᵗ

   _____

4. Saturday, January 31ˢᵗ

   _____

5. Friday, April 26ᵗʰ

   _____

D **Circle the letter of the correct answer.**

٢. ما هو تاريخ اليوم؟	١. ما اليوم؟
maa huwa tareekhul-yawm?	mal-yawm?
ا . اليوم إجازة	ا . أسبوع
alyawm 'ijaaza	'usbooᶜ
ب. اليوم ليس عندي أي شيء	ب. الإثنين
alyawm laysa ᶜindee 'ayy shay'	al'ithnayn
ج. اليوم هو ١٠ كانون الثاني	ج. تمّوز
alyawm huwa ᶜashara kanoon aththaani	tammooz
د. اليوم هو الأحد	د. شهر
alyawm huwaal-'aHad	shahr

The following questions are based on the dialogues presented in this unit. Review them before you choose your answers.

5. متى يدرس سماح كل اليوم؟
mata yadrus samaaH kullal-yawm?

ا. الأربعاء
al'arbiᶜaa'

ب. الثلاثاء
athulaathaa'

ج. الجمعة
aljumᶜa

د. الاثنين
al'ithnayn

6. من عنده يوم راحة؟
mann ᶜindahu yawm raaHa?

ا. ملحم
milHim

ب. رياض
riaaD

ج. رواد
rawaad

د. سماح
samaaH

3. ماذا يقول (.m) ملحم عن ٨ حزيران؟
maadha yaqool milHim ᶜann thamaanyia Hazeeraan?

ا. نهاية الأسبوع
nihaayatul 'usbooᶜ

ب. آذار
aadhaar

ج. عيد ميلاده
ᶜeed meelaaduhu

د. الثلاثاء
aththulaathaa'

4. ماذا يفعل (.m) زيد يوم الثلاثاء؟
maadha yafᶜal zayd yawmu-th thulaatha'?

ا. عنده كلب وهرتين
ᶜindahu kalb wahirratayn

ب. عنده امتحان الإنكليزية
ᶜindahu 'imtiHaanul-'ingleeziyya

ج. عنده بيت في السعودية
ᶜindahu bayt fis-saᶜoodiyya

د. له عائلة صغيرة
lahoo ᶜaa'ila Sagheera

E Match the Arabic words and expressions with their English equivalent.

A. yesterday

B. day after tomorrow

C. today

D. tomorrow

E. day before yesterday

1. _____ اليوم alyawm

2. _____ بعد غدا baᶜda ghadan

3. _____ قبل أمس qabla 'ams

4. _____ غدا ghadan

5. _____ أمس 'ams

F Write in Arabic.

1. the third month of the year _____

2. the month that brings May flowers _____

3. the first day of the Arabic week _____

4. the month of the national holiday in the United States _____

5. the month in which Halloween is celebrated _____

6. the month of your عيد ميلاد _____

G **Identify the English weekday according to the illustration.**

On Sunday, the first day of the week, Arab Christians go to mass. Monday is related to the number "2." In the same vein, the root for the word for Tuesday comes from the word for "3." On Wednesday girls and women in many Arab countries apply eyeliner and henna on their hands, after a bedouin custom. On Thursday children boil eggs, color them, and break them in a game. Friday is the day Muslims go to the mosque to hear a sermon and pray. "Light Saturday" is a day in the Christian calendar before Easter.

.1

_____

.2

_____

.3

_____

.4

_____

.5

_____

.6

_____

.7

_____

Read the paragraph; then select the correct answers.

هذا يوم خاص بالنسبة لرمزي (.m). رمزي سيذهب اليوم من الكويت
haadha yawmun khaaS binnisba liramzi. ramzy sayadhhabul-yawm minal-koowayt

إلى لبنان لزيارة صديقه ريمون (.m). إنه يوم السبت في التاسع من
'ilaa lubnaan liziyaarat Sadeeqahu reemoon. 'innahu yawmus-sabt fit-taasi‘ min

تشرين الثاني. إنه فصل الخريف والطقس جميل جدا اليوم.
tishreenath-thaani. 'innahu faSlul-khareef waTTaqs jameel jiddan al-yawm.

هو أيضا يوم نهائي أهم مباراة كرة قدم في العالم العربي
huwa 'ayDan yawm nihaa'iy 'ahamm mubaraat kurat qadam fil-‘aalamil-‘arabi

بين السعودية وتونس. الفريقان يلعبان في مدينة بيروت. عادة،
baynas-sa‘oodiyya watoonis. alfareeqaan yal‘abaan fee madeenat bayroot. ‘aadatan,

يكون من الصعب الحصول على تذاكر لهذه المباراة ولكن
yakoon minaS-Sa‘bil-HuSool ‘alaa tadhaakir lihaadhihil-mubaraat walaakin

لحسن الحظ رمزي وريمون معهما تذاكر. رمزي مسرور جدا اليوم.
lihusnil-HaDH ramzy wareemoon ma‘humaa tadhaakir. ramzy masroor
jiddan al-yawm.

teams	**fareeqaan**	فريقان	soccer championship	**mubaaraat kuratul-qadam**	مباراة كرة القدم
tickets	**tadhaakir**	تذاكر	important	**ahamm**	أهمّ
but	**laakin**	لكن	world	**al‘aalam**	العالم
luckily	**liHisnil-HaDHDH**	لحسن الحظ	are playing	**yal‘abaan**	يلعبان

ج. الثاني عشر من تشرين ثاني.
aththaani ‘ashar min tishreen thaani.

د. العشرون من تشرين ثاني
al‘ishroon min tishreen thaani

3. هو يوم خاص لرمزي.
huwa yamun khaas liramzi.

ا. نعم
na‘am

ب. لا
laa

ج. تقريبا
taqreeban

د. هو يوم عيد ميلاده
huwa yawm ‘eed meeladihi

1. ما اليوم؟
mal-yawm?

ا. الإثنين
alithnayn

ب. الجمعة
aljum‘a

ج. الثلاثاء
aththulaathaa'

د. السبت
assabt

2. ما التاريخ؟
mat-taareekh?

ا. العاشر من تشرين أول
al‘aashir min tishreen awwal

ب. التاسع من تشرين أول
attaasi‘ min tshreen 'awwal

4. من هو ريمون؟
mann huwa reemoon?

ج. السعودية
assaʿoodiyya

ا. أخو رمزي
'akhoo ramzy

د. الكويت
alkoowayt

ب. عم رمزي
ʿamm ramzy

6. كيف يشعر رمزي اليوم؟
kayfa yashʿur ramzil-yawm?

ج. أستاذ رمزي
'ustaadh ramzy

ا. مسرور
masroor

د. صديق رمزي
Sadeeq ramzy

ب. حزين
Hazeen

5. أي فريق يلعب ضد تونس؟
'ayy fareeq yalʿab Did toonis?

ج. غضبان
ghaDbaan

ا. لبنان
lubnaan

د. تعبان
Taʿbaan

ب. فلسطين
filasTeen

I لنتكلم! (*linatakallam!*) Find out the day or date your partner has each of the following. (Your teacher will explain how to use the two models.)

مثال:
mithaal:
Example:

test	'imtiHaan إمتحان	*What day is...?*	fee 'ayy yawm? في أي يوم؟
the holiday	al'ijaaza الإجازة	*When...?*	mata? متى؟
your birthday	ʿeed meeladak عيد ميلادك	*The birthday of....*	ʿeed meelaad.... عيد ميلاد.....
		music lesson	dars mooseeqa درس موسيقى

J دورك! (*dawrak!*) Find out whether you and your classmate know your days. You start by saying, «بعد غدا الأربعاء» Your classmate says, «اليوم الاثنين» You finish by saying, «غدا الثلاثاء» Then your partner goes back to: اليوم, etc. Continue until you have both identified all the days of the week.

Proverb

" الدهر يومان يوم لك ويوم عليك.
addahr yawmaan yawmun laka wayawmun ʿalayk.
Life is twofold, a time to give and a time to take. "

Using the Arabic Alphabet

In each row connect the letters to form words. Write each word in the blank box. Remember that the form of a letter may change, depending on its position in the word.

صفوف		ف	و	ف	ص	مثال Example
		ة	ف	ر	غ	1.
		ة	ق	ر	و	2.
		ب	ا	ت	ك	3.
		ر	ت	ف	د	4.
			م	ل	ق	5.
		ة	ق	ب	ط	6.
	ة	ا	ح	م	م	7.
	ة	ا	ر	ب	م	8.

Symtalk

K On the blank, write the correct word in Arabic.

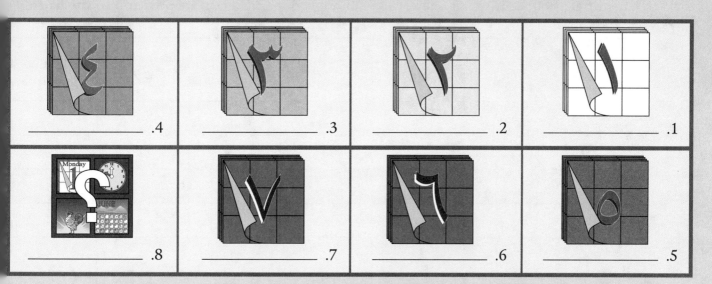

٤ _____ .4	٣ _____ .3	٢ _____ .2	١ _____ .1
_____ .8	٧ _____ .7	٦ _____ .6	٥ _____ .5

L Say the sentences, then write them in Arabic.

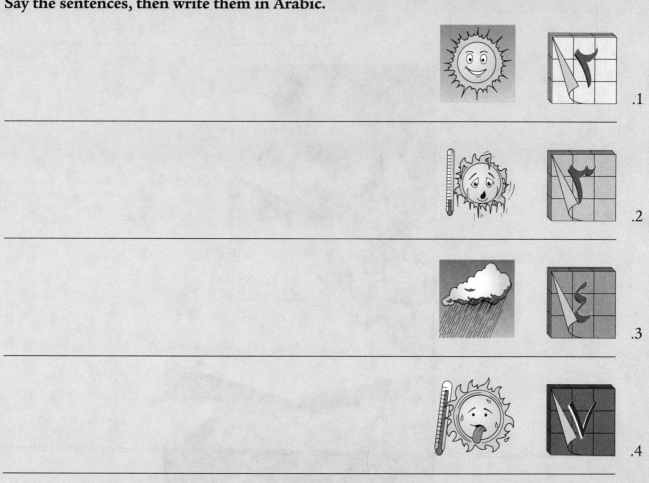

_____ .1

_____ .2

_____ .3

_____ .4

Work with a partner. Ask the question or give the answer. Then, write the dialogue.

_____

_____   .1

_____

_____   .2

_____

_____   .3

_____

_____   .4

_____

_____   .5

الثلاثاء

Mardi	Tuesday
20	**٢٠**

February 2007	شباط

عصر ٢,٥٩	٢	فجر ٤,٤٨
غروب ٥,٢٤	صفر	شروق ٦,١٩
عشاء ٦,٤٦	١٤٢٨	ظهر ١١,٥٢

ترعى العنزة حيث تُربط

January 2007 كانون الثاني

الأحد	السبت	الجمعة	الخميس	الأربعاء	الثلاثاء	الاثنين
7	6	5	4	3	2	1 رأس السنة الميلادية
14	13	12	11	10	9	8
21	20	19	18	17	16	15
28	27	26	25	24	23	22
				31	30	29

N **Look at the clippings to find the information requested below.**

1. Which holiday is mentioned on the January, 2007 calendar?

   _____

2. A. In the "Tuesday" clipping, circle the letter ظ and write it in the four positions:

Final	Medial	Initial	Independent

   B. In the same clipping, find the Arabic words for "sunrise" and "sunset." Write them.

   _____

   _____

Unit **17**

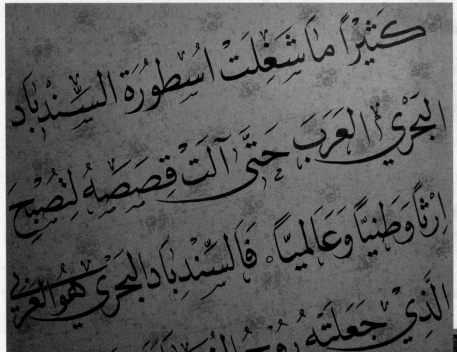

الأدب
al'adab
Literature

كَثِيراً ما شَغَلَتْ أُسْطُورَةُ السِّنْدِباد
البحرِيّ العَرَبَ حَتّى آلَتْ قِصَّتُهُ لِتُصْبِح
إِرْثاً وَطَنِيّاً وَعالَمِيّاً، فَالسِّنْدِباد البحرِيّ هُوَ العَرَبِيّ
الّذي جَعَلَتْهُ

225

Gibran Khalil Gibran (جبران خليل جبران) **jibraan khaleel jibraan (1883–1931)** Born to a poor family in Bsharri, a small town in northern Lebanon, Gibran immigrated to the United States at an early age with his siblings and mother. They resided in Boston, where Gibran and his family struggled to make a living. Through the help of a charity, the young Gibran had the opportunity to go to school, where he learned English. His study of English eventually led to a growing interest in art and literature. Writing for a local newspaper called *The Immigrant*, he made a name for himself. After returning to Beirut, he learned the Arabic language at *alHikma* School. He returned to the United States and became a notable author. His first Arabic work, which appeared in 1905, was followed by a collection of writings in both English and Arabic. In 1911, Gibran moved from Boston to New York, where he wrote his long novel *Broken Wings* (الأجنحة المتكسرة), as well as *The Storm* (العواصف). In New York he joined a number of Arab organizations where he worked diligently at promoting Arabic art and literature. A couple of years later, he opened an art studio, which permitted him to sell paintings as well as publish Arabic books. Later in New York he wrote his often-quoted book the *The Prophet* (النبي). Many people do not know that he coined the saying "Ask what you can do for your country, not what your country can do for you," which is usually attributed to John F. Kennedy. Gibran died in New York in 1931 and was buried in Lebanon. He is honored with a museum and a library in his hometown, Bsharri.

Najib Mahfouz (نجيب محفوظ) **najeeb mahfooDH (1911–2006)** One of the greatest Arab writers in recent history, Mahfouz won the Nobel Prize in Literature in 1988 for his achievement in creating "an Arabian narrative art that applies to all mankind." The entire Arab world took notice of Mahfouz's honor. Having written short stories in secondary school, he subsequently committed his life to writing novels. After graduating from what is known today as the University of Cairo, Mahfouz read the stories of prominent Arab authors like Tawfeek al-Hakeem and Taha

Husayn. He wrote over 45 novels and countless literary articles. In his novels he wrote about the daily life of Egyptians. His work reflects the socio-economic and cultural life of his contemporary native country. Many of his works have been made into movies or were translated into other media. Mahfouz held a number of positions in his life, including posts working for the government of Egypt for many years. He worked at the Ministry of Endowment ('awqaaf) and later as the director of art and film at another government agency. The last government job he held was as consultant for the Minister of Culture and Education in 1970. His novels have been translated into many languages, including English, French, German, Russian, and Italian. His most famous novels include *Midaq Alley* (زقاق المدق), *Adrift on the Nile* (ثرثرة فوق النيل), and *Mirrors* (المرايا).

Mai Ziadah (مي زيادة) **may ziyaada (1886–1941)** Ziadah was born in Palestine to a wealthy Lebanese father. She studied at the famous ʿaynToora School for Girls (مدرسة عينطورة), and moved to Egypt in 1907 to continue her education. A brilliant student and author, she learned five languages and published in three, in addition to Arabic. She read the famous Egyptian writers at the time but was very much influenced by the writing of Gibran, with whom she corresponded for two decades. Her first work, a collection of poems in French, was published in 1911. She followed that with three novels that she translated into Arabic from French, German, and English. In the early part of the 1920's, Ziadah authored six novels in Arabic considered to be the best work written by an Arab woman at the time. She did not have a happy ending to her life. While in Lebanon, a conspiracy by her relatives fueled by greed placed her in a mental hospital in Beirut. Many important personalities, like Amine Arrihaani, Adil Arslan, and Faris al-Khoury, pleaded for her release from the hospital. Upon release, she returned to Egypt, where she died. Her best novels include *Equality* (المساواة), which deals with social equality; *Words and Signals* (كلمات وإشارات), which deals with poverty and ways to help the poor; and *Between Ebb and Tide* (بين المد والجزر), a collection of poetry and prose on social issues.

Nizar Qabbani (نزار قباني) **nizaar qabbaani (1923–1998)** Born in Damascus, Qabbani was one of the most prominent Arab poets of the 20ᵗʰ century. During his life he lived in Syria, Lebanon, and England. In 1966, he settled permanently in Beirut, where he owned a publishing house. He wrote 41 volumes of poetry, considered to be among the best free verse ever written in Arabic. His early writing dealt with politics. He criticized the state of the Arab world in a very sharp tone, which prompted many politicians to call for his expulsion from Syria. He was so affected by the suicide of his sister, who had been living in a forced marriage that he made a commitment that through his poetry Arab women would be freed from the chains of tradition. He departed from political writing to devote a good portion of his life to writing about love. He became known as the "poet of love." While living in Lebanon, two tragedies engulfed his life once again, the death of his son at the age of 17 and later the death of his beloved wife, Balqees, who perished in an explosion at the Iraqi embassy where she was employed. Qabbani decided to leave Lebanon once and for all, shuttling between Paris, Geneva, and London. He spent the last 15 years of his life in London where once again he resumed writing political poetry. He died in London and was buried in Damascus. His most important love volumes are *The Brunette has Told Me* (قالت لي السمراء), *Drawing with Words* (الرسم بالكلمات). His most important political collections include *Margins on the Notebook of Setback* (هوامش على دفتر النكسة) and *When Will They Announce the Death of the Arabs?* (متى يعلنون وفاة العرب؟).

Tawfiq al-Hakim (توفيق الحكيم) **tawfeeq alHakeem (1898–1987)** Born in Alexandria, Egypt to a wealthy family, al-Hakim received his education in Cairo and Paris, where he studied law. In Paris he discovered his love of novels and plays. He visited a number of theatres and became influenced by Bernard Shaw. He returned to Egypt in 1930 and began his writing career. His first novel, *The Return of Spirit* (عودة الروح) made him famous. His work for the government as a District Attorney was the basis for his memoir *The Daily Memoir of a DA in Rural Egypt* (يوميات نائب في الأرياف). He became even more famous as a playwright, writing over 50 plays and earning the reputation as a playwright unmatched in Arabic literature. Some of his plays were published in *News Today*, a newspaper that he worked for in the '30's and '40's. A bachelor most of his life, he repudiated his reputation as the "enemy of women" by getting married. His most famous play is *People of the Cave* (أهل الكهف).

Abdul Wahhab al-Bayyati (عبد الوهاب البياتي) **ʻabdul-wahhaab albayyaati (1926–1999)** One of the last pioneers of modern Arabic poetry, al-Bayyati was born in Baghdad to a middle-class family. After graduating from college, he became a teacher of Arabic and later a journalist. He was sent to prison because of his political views, which prompted him to leave Iraq for Syria, Lebanon, then Egypt. Al-Bayyati spent a good portion of his life outside Iraq, in both the Arab world and Europe. He even lived in the Soviet Union from 1959–1964, where he became a professor at Moscow University. After moving back to Cairo, he continued writing poetry. In 1970 he moved to Spain, where he lived for ten years and became a popular writer, most of his writing having been translated into Spanish. After his sojourn in Spain, he went to Amman, Iraq, and later Syria, where he died. An author of over 30 volumes of Arabic poetry, many of which were translated into a number of languages, his most important works remain *Poetry in Exile* (أشعار في المنفى) and *Words Do Not Die* (كلمات لا تموت).

سعيد (.m): هل تحبين كتاب النبي لجبران خليل جبران؟

saʿeed: hal tuHibeen kitaab annaby lijibraan khaleel jibraan?

Said: Do you like *The Prophet* by Jibran Khalil Jibran?

أديبة (.f): نعم أحبه كثيرا. جبران أديب وشاعر لبناني عظيم.

'abeeba: naʿam 'uHibuhu katheeran. jibraan adeeb washaaʿr lubnaany ʿaDHeem.

Adeeba: Yes, I like him a lot. Jibran is a great Lebanese writer and poet.

أنيس (.m): من هو عبد الوهاب البياتي؟

'anees: mann huwa ʿabdul-wahhaabul-bayyaaty?

Anis: Who is Abdul Wahhab al-Bayyati?

سميرة (.f): هو شاعر عراقي مشهور جدا، وأنا قرأت قصائده.

sameera: huwa shaaʿir ʿiraaqy mashhoor jiddan, wa'anaa qara'tu qaSaa'idahu.

Samira: He's a very famous Iraqi poet and I read his odes.

طلال (.m): هل مي زيادة لبنانية أو مصرية؟

Talaal: hal may ziaadah lubnaaniyya 'aw maSriyya?

Talal: Is Mai Ziyadeh Lebanese or Egyptian?

أميرة (.f): هي تقول أنها لبنانية وفلسطينية ومصرية.

'ameera: hiya taqool 'annaha lubnaaniyya wafalasTeeniyya wamaSraiyya.

Amira: She says that she is Lebanese, Palestinian, and Egyptian.

هشام (.m): هل تحبين قراءة كتب نثرية أو شعرية؟

hishaam: hal tuHibeen qiraa'at kutub nathriyya 'aw shiʿriyya?

Hisham: Do like to read prose or poetry books?

أليشا (.f): أنا لا أحب قراءة الكتب. أحب قراءة المجلات والجرائد فقط.

'aleesha: 'anaa laa 'uHibu qiraa'atal-kutub. 'uHibu qiraa'atal-majallaat waljaraa'id faqaT.

Alicia: I do not like to read books. I like to read magazines and newspapers only.

أديب (.m): هل قرأت قصة نجيب محفوظ الجديدة؟

'adeeb: hal qara'ti qiSSat najeeb maHfooDH aljadeeda?

Adib: Did you reed Najeeb Mahfouz's new story?

منية (.f): نعم، قرأت القصة الأسبوع الماضي. هي ممتازة.

munya: naʿam, qar'atul-qiSSa al'usbooʿal-maaDy. hiya mumtaaza.

Monia: Yes, I read the story last week. It is excellent.

رجاء (.f): هل توفيق الحكيم كاتب أو شاعر؟

rajaa': hal tawfeeq'al-Hakeem kaatib 'aw shaaʿir?

Rajaa: Is Tawfeeq al-Hakim a writer or a poet?

شادي (m.): هو كاتب مسرحي كبير، كتب حوالي خمسين مسرحية.

shaady: huwa kaatib masraHy kabeer, kataba Hawaali-khamseen masraHiyya.

Shadi: He is a big playwright, and wrote about 50 plays.

عماد (m.): أنا أحب نزار قباني كثيرا.

'imaad: 'anaa 'uHibu nizaar qabbaany katheeran.

Imad: I like Nizar Qabbani a lot.

عبير (f.): وأنا أيضا، أحب كتاب الرسم بالكلمات.

ᶜabeer: wa'anaa 'ayDan, 'uHibu kitaab arrasim bilkalimaat.

Abir: Me too, I like the book arrasim bilkalimaat.

Activities نشاطات

nashaaTaat

A **Identify who. . .**

1. . . .was educated in France and Egypt.

_____

2. . . .opened an art studio in New York.

_____

3. . . .is known to be the "poet of love."

_____

4. . . .communicated with Gibran for two decades.

_____

5. . . .was born in Damascus and died in London.

_____

6. . . .studied English in Boston and Arabic at *Darul –Hikma* in Beirut.

_____

B **Match the names on the right with the descriptions on the left.**

A. Syrian poet	najeeb mahfooDH نجيب محفوظ _____ .1
B. Iraqi Poet	may ziyaada مي زيادة _____ .2
C. author of *The Prophet*	jibraan khaleel jibraan جبران خليل جبران _____ .3
D. worked as a District Attorney	tawfeeq alHakeem توفيق الحكيم _____ .4
E. was accused of insanity	nizaar qabbaani نزار قباني _____ .5
F. wrote the famous *Adrift on the Nile*	ᶜabdul-wahhab al-bayyati. عبد الوهاب البياتي _____ .6

C

In Arabic, write the full name of the author of each work listed below.

١. الأجنحة المتكسرة

al'ajniHal-mutakassira

_____

٢. زقاق المدق

zuqaaqul-midaq

_____

٣. المساواة

almusaawaat

_____

٤. يوميات نائب في الأرياف

yawmiyyaat naa'ib fil-'aryaaf

_____

٥. الرسم بالكلمات

arrasmu-bilkalimaat

_____

شاعر	أديب	كاتب	ناقد
shaaᶜir	**'adeeb**	**kaatib**	**naaqid**
poet	literary	writer	critic
شعر	نثر	صحافي	
shiᶜr	**nathr**	**SaHaafi**	
poetry	prose	journalist	

D

In Arabic, what do you call the person or thing that. . .

_____

١. ...يكتب الشعر؟

...yaktubush shiᶜr?

_____

٢. ...يكتب في جريدة؟

...yaktub fee jareeda?

_____

٣. ...يكتب النثر؟

...yaktubun nathr?

_____

٤. ...يكتب؟

...yaktub?

_____

٥. ...ينقد الأدب والشعر؟

...yanqudul 'adab washshiᶜr?

Match each book title with the name of the author who wrote it.

A. Najib Mahfouz

_____ .1

B. Khalil Gibran

_____ .2

C. Nizar Qabbani

_____ .3

D. May Ziyaada

_____ .4

E. Tawfeeq al-Hakim

_____ .5

F. Abdul Wahhab al-Bayyati

_____ .6

F Which author or authors would most likely. . .

1. . . .know a lot about painting and framing pictures?

_____

2. . . .know about theatre and stage?

_____

3. . . .know about foreign languages?

_____

4. . . .know about the social life of Egyptians?

_____

5. . . .liberate women from traditions?

_____

G In Arabic, write the name of the birthplace of the author who wrote:

1. النبي annabi

_____

2. كلمات لا تموت kalimaat la tamoot

_____

3. هوامش على دفتر النكسة hawaamish ʿala daftarin-naksa

_____

4. ثرثرة فوق النيل tharthara fawqan-neel

_____

5. بين المد والجزر baynal-maddi-waljazr

_____

H Complete the sentences with the names of the authors.

1. _____ wrote poems about politics and love.
2. _____ wrote about rural life in Egypt.
3. _____ wrote about equality between social groups.
4. _____ worked as a professor at a European university.
5. _____ wrote about social equality and other social issues.
6. _____ is honored in both the U.S. and Lebanon.
7. _____ lost his sister, son, and wife during his lifetime.
8. _____ worked as a consultant for a governmental minister.
9. _____ received her education at ʿaynToora School for Girls.
10. _____ learned English in Boston.

I **Fill in the blank with the name of the appropriate character from the dialogues.**

1. _____ likes to read magazines and newspapers.

2. _____ read Mahfouz's new story.

3. _____ likes Khalil Gibran.

4. _____ reads Al-bayyaati's poems.

5. _____ likes to read Nizar Qabbani.

6. _____ is asking about Tawfeeq al-Hakeem.

7. _____ says that May Ziaadah is Lebanese, Egyptian, and Palestinian.

J دورك! *(dawrak!)* **Choose one of the novels mentioned in this unit. Ask the librarian for help you find the book and / or information about the plot, or do some research on the Internet. Look over carefully what you have found, and then, in your own words, retell the story to your classmates. You may wish to use visuals to relay the story and the names of the important characters.**

Proverb

" القلم أقوى من السيف.
alqalam 'aqwa minas-sayf.
The pen is mightier than the sword. "

Using the Arabic Alphabet

In each row connect the letters to form words. Write the words in the blank box.
Remember that the form of a letter may change, depending on its position in the word.

	بيروت	ت	و	ر	ي	ب	مثال Example
				ق	ش	م	د	.1
		ة	ر	ه	ا	ق	ل	ا	.2
			ض	ا	ي	ر	ل	ا	.3
		ة	م	ا	ن	م	ل	ا	.4
				ط	ق	س	م	.5
			ش	ك	ا	ر	م	.6
			ي	ز	ا	غ	ن	ب	.7
		م	و	ط	ر	خ	ل	ا	.8
			ء	ا	ن	ع	ص	.9
					ي	ب	ظ	.10
		ة	ح	و	د	ل	ا	.11

235   Literature   Unit 17

Symtalk

K In the space, write the correct word or expression in Arabic.

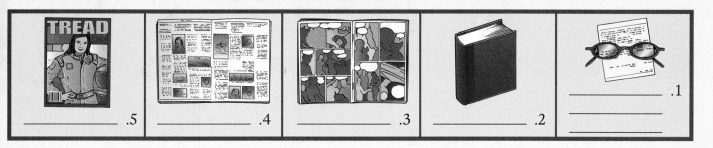

_____ .5   _____ .4   _____ .3   _____ .2   _____ .1
                                                                _____

L Say the following sentences, then write them.

    .1

_____

     .2

_____

           .3

_____

     .4

_____

.1

_____

_____

_____

_____

_____

.2

_____

_____

_____

_____

_____

.3

_____

_____

_____

_____

.4

_____

_____

_____

_____

_____

 Look at the clippings to find the information requested below.

1. For the clipping الآن في المكتبات, name one title and translate it into English.

   _____

2. In the clipping الموسوعة العربية العالمية the first bullet states that "the source is a must for home, school, work, library, student, researcher." What is the Arabic name of the source?

   _____

Unit 18

الراحة والاستجمام

arraaHa wal'istijmaam

Leisure and Recreation

إلى أين أنت ذاهب / ذاهبة؟
'ila 'ayna 'anta dhaahib / dhaahiba?
Where are you going?

أنا ذاهب إلى المباراة.
'anaa dhaahib 'ilal-mubaaraat.
I'm going to the game.

أنا ذاهب إلى المتحف.
'anaa dhaahib 'ilal-matHaf.
I'm going to the museum.

أنا ذاهب إلى الحفلة.
'anaa dhaahib 'ilal-Hafla.
I'm going to the party.

أنا ذاهبة إلى البحر.
'anaa dhaahiba 'ilal-baHr.
I'm going to the beach.

إلى أين ستذهب الليلة؟ **maysam: 'ila 'ayna satadhhabul-layla?** ميسم (f.):	Where are you going to go tonight?
أنا سأذهب إلى المباراة. **makram: 'anaa sa'adhhab 'ilal-mubaaraat.** مكرم (m.):	I'm going to go to the game.
وأنا أيضاً! **wa'anaa 'ayDan!** ميسم:	Me too!

❀ ❀ ❀ ❀

إلى أين ستذهبين اليوم؟ **rabeeᶜ: 'ila 'ayna satadhhabeenal-yawm?** ربيع (m.):	Where are you going today?
أنا سأذهب إلى المتحف إلى المتحف الوطني. ربيعة (f.):	

rabeeᶜa: 'anaa sa'adhhab 'ilal-matHaf... 'ilal-matHafil-waTani.
I'm going to go to the museum... to the National Museum.

لماذا؟ **rabeeᶜ: limaadha?** ربيع:	Why?
لأرى معرض صور جبران. ربيعة:	

rabeeᶜa: li'araa maᶜraD Sowar jibraan.
To see the Gibran exhibit.

The future is formed by adding the prefix سـ (sa) to any present tense verb.
For example: يذهب سيذهب
yadhhab   sayadhhab
he goes   he will go, is going to go

ألعب الكرة الطائرة.
'al°abul-kuraT-Taa'ira.
I play volleyball.

ألعب كرة القدم.
'al°abu kuratal-qadam.
I play soccer.

أي رياضة تلعب؟
'ayy riaaDa tal°ab?
What sports do you play?

ألعب كرة المضرب.
al°abu kuratal-maDrab.
I play tennis.

ألعب كرة السلة.
'al°abu kuratas-salla.
I play basketball.

ألعب كرة القاعدة.
'al°abu kuratal-qaa°ida.
I play baseball.

ألعب كرة القدم الآميركية.
'al°ab kurat-alqadam al'amreekiyya.
I play American football.

أحب التزلّج.
'uHibbut-tazalluj.
I like skiing.

ماذا تحب أن تفعل؟
maadha tuHib 'an tafᶜal?
What do you like to do?

أحب الرقص.
'uHibbur-raqS.
I like dancing.

أحب القراءة.
'uHibbul-qiraa'a.
I like reading.

أحب ركوب الخيل.
'uHibbu rukoobal-khayl.
I like horseback riding.

أحب السباحة.
'uHibbus-sibaaHa.
I like swimming.

أحب ركوب الدراجة.
'uHibbu rukoobad-darraaja.
I like biking.

أحب أن ألعب كرة القدم الآميركية.
I like to play American football.   'uHib an alᶜab kurat-alqadam al'amreekiyya.

There's a picnic tomorrow. riHaab: hunaaka biknik ghadan.	هناك بكنك غدا. :(f.) رحاب
Where? muHammad: 'ila 'ayna?	إلى أين؟ :(m.) محمد
riHaab: 'ilash-shaaTi'. hal tureedudh-dhihaab maᶜee?	إلى الشاطئ هل تريد الذهاب معي؟ :رحاب
At the beach. Do you want to go with me?	
Yes, I love swimming. muHammad: naᶜam, 'anaa 'uHibus-sibaaHa.	نعم أنا أحب السباحة. :محمد

❀❀❀❀❀

Are you going to the party tonight? reeta: hal satadhhab 'ilal-Haflal-layla?	هل ستذهب إلى الحفلة الليلة؟ :(f.) ريتا
Of course. There'll be music, won't there? Tooni: Tabᶜan. 'alaa sayakoon hunaak mooseeqa?	طبعا ألا سيكون هناك موسيقى؟ :(m.) طوني
Yes, I love to dance! reeta: naᶜam, 'anaa 'uHibur-raqS!	نعم، أنا أحب الرقص! :ريتا

Activities نشاطات

nashaaTaat

A Where are you going? Complete each sentence in Arabic, using the cues in parentheses.

1. أذهب إلى _____ (game)
   'adhhab 'ila....

2. أذهب إلى _____ (picnic)
   'adhhab 'ila....

3. أذهب إلى _____ (museum)
   'adhhab 'ila....

4. أذهب إلى _____ (beach)
   'adhhab 'ila....

5. أذهب إلى _____ (party)
   'adhhab 'ila....

B The following questions are based on the dialogues presented in this unit. Refer to them before circling the correct answer.

1. متى المباراة؟ matal-mubaaraat?

   ا. غدا ghadan

   ب. الجمعة aljumᶜa

   ج. الليلة allayla

   د. بعد غدا baᶜda ghadan

2. ما هو "الوطني"؟ maa huwal-waTani?

   ا. حصان HiSaan

   ب. مباراة mubaaraat

   ج. معرض فني maᶜraD fanny

   د. متحف matHaf

3. من هو جبران؟ mann huwa jibraan?

   ا. أستاذ فن 'ustaadh fann

   ب. فنان عربي fannaan ᶜarabi

   ج. مدير متحف mudeer matHaf

   د. ممثّل عربي mumaththil ᶜarabi

4. متى البكنك؟ matal-biknik?

   ا. غدا ghadan

   ب. اليوم alyawm

   ج. بعد غدا baᶜda ghadan

   د. أمس 'ams

5. أين البكنك؟ 'aynal-biknik?

   ا. في بيروت fee bayroot

   ب. في المتحف fil-matHaf

   ج. في الحديقة fil-Hadeeqa

   د. على الشاطئ ᶜalash-shaaTiᶜ

C

What sports do you play? Complete each sentence in Arabic.

1. ألعب _____.
'al°ab....

2. ألعب _____.
'al°ab....

3. ألعب _____.
'al°ab....

4. ألعب _____.
'al°ab....

5. ألعب _____.
'al°ab....

D

What do you like to do? Complete each sentence in Arabic.

1. أحب أن _____.
'uHibu 'an....

2. أحب أن _____.
'uHibu 'an....

3. أحب أن _____.
'uHibu 'an....

4. أحب أن _____.
'uHibu 'an....

5. أحب أن _____.
'uHibu 'an....

6. أحب أن _____.
'uHibu 'an....

7. أحب أن _____.
'uHibu 'an....

E

Complete the dialogue in Arabic.

سميرة (.f): إلى أين (1.) _____ اليوم؟

sameera: 'ila 'ayn... alyawm?

أميرة (.f): أنا ذاهبة (2.) _____ الشاطئ. هل تريدين (3.) _____ معي؟

'ameera: 'anaa dhaahiba.... shaaTi'. hal tureedeen... ma'ee?

سميرة: (4.) _____ أنا أحب الشاطئ.

sameera: ...'anaa 'uHibush shaaTi'.

أميرة: وأنا (5.) _____ ! ماذا تريدين أن تفعلي هناك؟

'ameera: wa'ana...! maadhaa tureedeen 'an taf'ali hunaak?

سميرة: أحب (6.) _____ ألعب الكرة الطائرة.

sameera: 'uHibu... 'al'abul kuraT-Taa'ira.

أميرة: أنا أحب (7.) _____ في البحر.

'ameera: 'anaa 'uHibu... fil baHr.

F

Read the paragraph; then circle the best answer to each question on the next page.

ندينّ (.f) تنظّم حفلة صغيرة على الشاطئ بسبب عيد ميلادها. يصبح
nadeen tunaDHim Hafla Sagheera 'alash-shaaTi' bisabab 'eed meelaadiha. yuSbiH

عمرها إثنا عشرة سنة اليوم. سوف تدعو الأصدقاء باسم (.m) وجاد (.m)
'umruha 'ithnaa 'ashrata sanal-yawm. sawfa tad'ool-'aSdiqaa' baasim wajaad

وسالي (.f) وغازي (.m) إلى الحفلة. تبدأ الحفلة في الساعة الثالثة. الجو حار ولطيف جدا.
wasaaly waghaazy 'ilal Hafla. tabda'ul-Hafla fis-saa'ati thaalitha. 'aljaww Haar walaTeef jiddan.

أصدقاؤها يحبون لعب الكرة الطائرة والسباحة في البحر. بعد
'aSdiqaa'uha yuHibboon la'ibal-kuraT-Taa'ira wassibaaHa fil-baHr. ba'da

مباراة الكرة الطائرة، الأولاد يكونون جائعين جدا. سوف يكون هناك
mubaaraatil-kuraT-Taa'ira, 'al'awlaad yakoonoon jaa'i'een jiddan. sawfa yakoon hunaak

ساندويشات ومشروبات وطبعا البوظة وقالب حلوى عيد ميلادها.
sandweeshaat wamashroobaat waTab'an albooDHa waqaalib Halwa 'eed meelaadiha

حفلة عيد ميلادها عل الشاطئ ستكون مدهشة! ندين سعيدة جدا.
Haflat 'eed meelaadiha 'alash-shaaTi' satakoon mudhisha! nadeen sa'eeda jiddan.

starts	**tabda'**	تبدأ	organizing	**tunaDHDHim**	تنظم
pleasant	**laTeef**	لطيف	because of	**bisabab**	بسبب
after	**ba'd**	بعد	turning	**yuSfiH**	يصبح
be	**yakoon**	يكون	will	**sawfa**	سوف

١. كم يبلغ عمر (f.) عمر ندين اليوم...؟
kamm yablugh ʿumr nadeen alyawm...?

أ. ١٤ arbaʿata ʿashar
ب. ١٣ thalaathata ʿashar
ج. ١٢ 'ithnaa ʿashar
د. ١١ 'iHdaa ʿashar

٢. في أي ساعة تبدأ الحفلة...؟
fee 'ayy saʿa tabda'ul-Hafla...?

أ. في الساعة الخامسة fis-saaʿal-khaamisa
ب. في الساعة الثالثة fis-saaʿath-thaalitha
ج. في الساعة الرابعة fis-saaʿar-raabiʿa
د. في الساعة الثانية fis-saaʿa-thaaniya

٣. كيف الجوّ...؟
kayfal-jaww...?

أ. الجو جميل aljaww jameel
ب. الجو مثلج aljaww muthlij
ج. الجو ممطر aljaww mumTir
د. الجو عاطل aljaww ʿaaTil

٤. الأولاد يحبون أن يلعبوا رياضة....
al'awlaad yuHiboon 'an yalʿaboo riyaaDat....

أ. كرة السلة kuratus-salla
ب. كرة القاعدة kuratul-qaaʿida
ج. الكرة الطائرة alkuraT-Taa'ira
د. كرة القدم kuratul-qadam

٥. ماذا سيأكل الأولاد...؟
madhaa saya'kulul-'awlaad...?

أ. قالب حلوى qaalib Halwa
ب. شاطئ 'shaaTi
ج. مطعم maTʿam
د. حفلة Hafla

G دورك! (dawrak!) Try this word association game with a partner. Each of you writes a list of five nouns from this unit. Exchange lists with a partner. Within a time frame decided by the teacher, your partner will have to say a word that is related to each noun, for example, كتاب ، قراءة / متحف ، فنون. If your partner successfully offers a related word within the time frame, he or she earns a gold star or a prize from the grab bag. If not, or when the time is up, it is your turn.

H لنتكلّم! (*linatakallam!*) Think of three places where you could go this weekend, such as a museum, a beach, a picnic. Your partner will ask you where you are going to go and you should answer appropriately. Then reverse the roles, using new places.

مثال:
mithaal:
Example:

A: إلى أين ستذهب؟ ('ilaa 'ayna satadhhab?)

B: سأذهب إلى الشاطئ (sa'adhhab 'ilash-shaaTi')

Proverb

"" كل شمس لها مغيب.
kull shams laha magheeb.
Every sunrise has a sunset. ""

Using the Arabic Alphabet

In each row connect the letters to form words. Write the words in the blank box.
Remember that the form of a letter may change, depending on its position in the word.

	لبنان	ن	ا	ن	ب	ل	مثال Example
		ا	ي	ر	و	س	.1
	ن	د	ر	أ	ل	ا	.2
	ن	ي	ط	س	ل	ف	.3
	ق	ا	ر	ع	ل	ا	.4
	ت	ي	و	ك	ل	ا	.5

Symtalk

I   In the space, write the correct word or expression in Arabic.

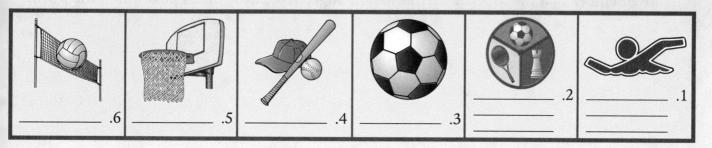

J   Say the sentences, then write them in Arabic.

     .1

_____

     .2

_____

         .3

_____

   .4

_____

         .5

_____

Work with a partner. Ask the question or give the answer. Then, write the dialogue.

.1

_____

_____   _____

.2

_____

_____   _____

.3

_____

_____   _____

.4

_____

_____   _____

An exquisite resort style hotel where elegance and spectacular mountains and city view meet, featuring one of the finest 'KASR EL WADI' Restaurants.

مطعم قصر الوادي ـ حيث تلقى اشهى المأكولات والمناظر الخلابة

Ain el-Hassa Avenue - Hammana, Lebanon • Tel: +961 5 531 444 • Fax: +961 5 531 936
E-mail: info@valleyviewhotels.com • http://www.valleyviewhotels.com

L **Look at the clippings to find the information requested below.**

1. In the clipping with the building that has a red roof, what is being advertised?

   _____

2. In the ad about the roller coaster, for how many days does the carnival last?

   _____

Unit 19

التسوّق
attasawwuq
Shopping

أتسوّق.... / أتبضّع....
'atasawwaq / 'atabaDDa^c....
I shop....

محلات شادي
maHallaat shaady

مكتبة شادي
maktabat shady

الزبون
azzuboon
customer

البائع
albaa'i^c
salesclerk

حذاء رياضة
Hidhaa' riyaaDa
athletic shoes

...في المجمّع التجار ي.
...fil-majamma^cit-tijaari.
...at the shopping center (mall).

albaa'i^c:	marHaba, hal yumkinuni musaa^cadatuki?	البائع (.m): مرحبا، هل يمكنني مساعدتك؟
Salesclerk:	Hello, Ma'am. May I help you?	
azzaboona:	laa, shukran. 'anaa 'atafarraj faqaT.	الزبونة (.f): لا، شكرا. أنا أتفرّج فقط.
Customer:	No, thanks. I'm just looking.	

❀✿❀✿❀

albaa'i^c:	SabaHul khayr sayyidati. hal yumkinuni musaa^cadatuki?	البائع: صباح الخير، سيّدتي. هل يمكنني مساعدتك؟
	Good morning, Sir. May I help you?	
azzaboona:	na^cam. 'uHibbu 'an 'ashtari kitaaban.	الزبونة: نعم. أحب أن أشتري كتابا.
	Yes. I'd like to buy a book.	
albaa'i^c:	Hasanan. ^cindana majmoo^ca kabeera.	البائع: حسنا. عندنا مجموعة كبيرة.
	Fine. We have a large selection.	

❀✿❀✿❀

saamy:	'ila 'ayna 'anti dhaahiba?	سامي (.m): إلى أين أنت ذاهبة؟
Sami:	Where are you going?	
saamiya:	'ilal-mujamma^cit-tijaari.	سامية (.f): إلى المجمع التجاري
Samia:	To the shopping center.	
What are you going to buy?	**maadha satashtareen?**	سامي: ماذا ستشترين؟
Athletic shoes.	**Hidhaa' riyaaDa.**	سامية: حذاء رياضة.

...في الدكان	في الدكان	
...fid-dukkaan		
...at the store		

أمين الصندوق/ محاسب
'ameenuS-Sandooq / muHaasib
cashier

نقود
nuqood
bills

فلوس
fuloos
money (bills or paper money)

زبون
zuboon
customer

أسطوانة / قرص
'usTuwaana / qurS
compact disk / CD

الصندوق
aSSandooq
cash register

نقود حجرية
nuqood Hajariyya
coins

تنزيلات
tanzeelaat
Sale

azzaboon:	bikamm haadhal-qurS?	بكم هذا القرص؟	:(.m) الزبون
Customer:	How much is this compact disc?		
almuHaasiba:	bikhamsata ᶜashar leera.	بخمسة عشر ليرة.	:(.f) المحاسبة
Cashier:	It costs 15.00 pounds.		
azzaboon:	haadha ghaaly qaleelan!	هذا غالي قليلا!	الزبون:
	That's a little expensive!		
almuHaasiba:	laa, haadha rakheeS.	لا، هذا رخيص.	المحاسبة:
	No, it's cheap.		
azzaboon:	Hasanan, sa'ashtareeha. tafaDDali ya 'aanisa.	حسنا، سأشتريها. تفضّلي يا آنسة.	الزبون:
	Okay. I'll buy it. There you are, Miss.		
almuHaasiba:	shukran jazeelan, haadhihi Siraafa lak.	شكرا جزيلا، هذه صرافة لك.	المحاسبة:
	Thank you very much. Here's your change.		

بائع
baaᶜiᶜ
vendor

لوبيا
loobiya
green or string beans

درّاق
durraaq
peaches

...في السوق
...fis-sooq
...at the market

baaᶜi:	'ayy shay' 'aakhar?	أي شيء آخر؟	بائع:
Salesclerk:	Anything else?		
azzaboon:	aah, thalaath banadooraaw khams durraaqaat waqaleel	آه، ثلاث بندورات خمس	الزبون:
	minal-loobiya. naᶜam haadha kul shay'.	دراقات وقليل من اللوبيا. نعم، هذا كل شيء.	
Customer:	Three tomatoes, five peaches,		
	and some string beans. Yes, that's all.		

Extra Vocabulary مفردات إضافيّة

mufradaat iDaafiyya

alkulfa الكلفة the cost	lisharaa' لشراء to buy
aththaman huwa الثمن هو it costs	'ashtari أشتري I'm buying or I buy
thamanuha ثمنها it costs	littabaDDu^c للتبضع to shop (make purchases)

Activities نشاطات

nashaaTaat

A Match the items for sale on the right with the stores in which they can be found on the left.

A. market

B. shoe store

C. furniture store

D. stationery store

E. music store

1. _____ حذاء تنس Hidhaa' tanis

2. _____ لوبيا loobiya

3. _____ أقراص 'aqraaS

4. _____ طاولات وكراسي Taawilaat wakaraasy

5. _____ أقلام ودفاتر 'aqlaam wadafaatir

B Complete each sentence according to the illustration.

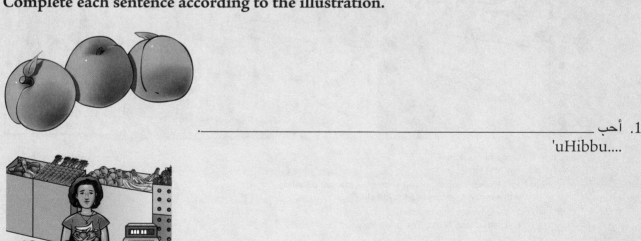

1. أحب _____.
   'uHibbu....

2. السيدة أم هشام تشتري بعض الفواكه من _____.
   assayyida 'umm hishaam tashtari ba^cDal fawaakih min....

٣. أشتري كل حاجياتي من _____
'ashtari kull Haajiyaati min....

٤. هذه _____ سيّدي.
haadhihi... sayyidi.

٥. القرص رخيص _____ ثلاث ليرات فقط.
alqurS rakheeS... thalaath leeraat faqaT.

C Choose the word from the following list that completes each sentence correctly.

لشراء	الـ	دكان	ليرات	رخيصة
lisharaa'	al	dukkaan	leeraat	rakheesa

مالك (.m) سيذهب إلى (1.) _____ الموسيقى. (2.) _____ أسطوانة موسيقى

maalik sayadhhab 'ila... almooseeqa... 'usTuwaanat mooseeqa

كلاسيكية. هناك أسطوانة لفريد الأطرش. ثمنها عشرة (3.) _____ ليست

klaaseekiyya. hunaaka 'usTuwaana lifareedil-'aTrash. thamanuha ʿashrat.... laysat

غالية. هي (4.) _____ مالك سيشتري (5.) _____ أسطوانة.

ghaaliya. hiya.... maalik sayashtari... 'usTuwaana

D Circle the correct answers.

1. If you see the sign تنزيلات (*tanzeelaat*), how would you expect the price of the object to be?

   A. رخيص
   rakheeS

   B. فلوس
   fuloos

   C. غالي
   ghaali

   D. صرافة / فراطة
   Siraafa / firaaTa

2. What do you reply if the cashier says "ثمنها تسعون ليرة" ("*thamanuha tisʿoon leera*")?

   A. تفضّل.
   tafaDDal.

   B. بكم السعر؟
   bikamis-siʿr?

   C. أين السوق؟
   'aynas-sooq?

   D. شكرا، هذا كل شيء.
   shukran, haadha kull shay'.

3. What do you get back if you give the cashier too much money?

   A. صندوق
   Sandooq

   B. مجمّع تجاري
   mujammaʿattijaari

   C. فلوس
   fuloos

   D. صرافة / فراطة
   Siraafa / firaaTa

4. Who helps you find what you need?

   A. دراق
   durraaq

   B. البائع
   albaa'iʿ

   C. المحاسبة
   almuHaasiba

   D. الزبون
   azzaboon

5. What do you say if you don't need the salesclerk's help right now?

   A. هل يمكنني مساعدتك؟
   hal yumkinuni musaaʿadatuk?

   B. غالية قليلا؟
   ghaaliya qaleelan?

   C. أتفرّج فقط، شكرا.
   'atafarraj faqaT.

   D. أي شيء آخر؟
   'ayy shay' aakhar?

E Write the following sentences in English.

1. أشتري حذاء رياضة. 'ashtari Hidhaa' riyaaDa.

_____

2. أنت تشتري سبع دراقات. 'anta tashtari sabʿa durraaqaat.

_____

3. هي تشتري أسطوانة. hiya tashtari 'usTuwaana.

_____

F. Circle the correct answer for each question.

١. هل هذا كل شيء؟
hal haadha kull shay'?

ا. لا، رخيصة.
laa, rakheeSa.

ب. لا، قليل من الدراق من فضلك.
laa, qaleel minad-durraaq min faDlak.

ج. أنا أتفرّج فقط.
'anaa 'atafarraj faqaT.

د. اغال.
aghaal.

ج. نعم، هذا كل شيء.
naᶜam, haadha kull shay'.

د. لا، هو غالي.
laa, huwa ghaaliy.

٢. لماذا تذهب إلى الدكان؟
limaadha tadhab 'ilad-dukkan?

ا. القرص سعره خمسة عشر ليرة.
alqurS siᶜruhu khamsat ᶜashar leera.

ب. ليس معي فلوس كثيرة.
laysa maᶜi fuloos katheera.

ج. أريد أن أشتري كتابا.
'ureedu 'an 'ashtariy kitaaban.

د. الزبون يتكلّم مع البائع.
azzuboon yatakallam maᶜal-baa'iᶜ.

٣. هل حذاء الرياضة رخيص؟
hal Hidhaa'ur-riyaaDa rakheeS?

ا. نعم، معي الفلوس.
naᶜam, maᶜil-fuloos.

ب. لا، هو البائع.
laa, huwal baa'iᶜ.

٤. بكم سعر القرص؟
bikam siᶜrul-qurS?

ا. سعره خمسة عشر ليرة.
siᶜruhu khamsat ᶜashar leera.

ب. الصندوق هنا.
aSSundooq huna.

ج. لا، غالي.
laa, ghaaly.

د. هي في المجمّع التجاري.
hiya fil mujammaᶜut-tijaari.

٥. ماذا ستشتري؟
maadha satashtari?

ا. السوق.
assooq.

ب. الصندوق.
aSSundooq.

ج. بندورة.
banadoora.

د. نقود حجريّة.
nuqood Hajariyya.

G. Majeed is shopping in a clothing store. Complete his conversation with the salesclerk.

البائع: نهارك سعيد يا سيدي. هل يمكنني (1.) _____؟
albaa'iᶜ: nahaarak saᶜeed ya sayyidi. hal yumkinuni...?

مجيد: أنا (2.) _____ فقط.
majeed: 'anaa... faqaT.

البائع: عندنا تنزيلات. كل شيء (3.)_____. قمصان ، بنطلونات ، جاكيتات ، أحذية.
albaa'iᶜ: ᶜindana tanzeelaat. kull shay'... qumSaan, banTaloonat, jakitaat, 'aHdhiya.

مجيد: شكرا لك سيدي. حسنا، بكم (4.) _____ هذا البنطلون الأزرق؟
majeed: shukran laka sayyidi. Hasanan, bikam... haadhal bantaloon al'azraq?

البائع: سعره ثلاثون دينارا.
albaa'iᶜ: siᶜruhu thalaathoon deenaaran.

مجيد: هذا (5.) _____ قليلا. لا يمكنني شراء البنطلون. ليس معي ثلاثون دينارا.
majeed: haadha... qaleelan. laa, yumkinuni sharaa'al-bantaloon. laysa maᶜi thalaathoon deenaaran.

H لنتكلّم! (*linatakallam!*) Think of three things you would like to buy (for example, a notebook, a shirt, a sandwich). Ask your partner how much each one costs: بكم سعر؟ (*bikam si'r?*) He / she should tell you a specific price in pounds. Then react to the price by saying هذا رخيص (*haadha rakheeS*), هذا غالي (*haadha ghaaly*), or هذا جيّد (*haadha jayyid*).

I دورك! (*dawrak!*) You and your partner are going to role-play a situation in a store. One of you is the customer and the other is the salesclerk. The salesclerk greets the customer and offers help. The customer says that he / she wants to buy a certain item. The salesclerk mentions the large selection of those items. The customer asks how much the item costs. The clerk helps with the purchase, thanks the customer, and says good-bye. Use props, such as a

مسطرة، دفتر، قرص أو أسطوانة، كنزه، كتاب، قلم، تفاحة، الخ
(*masTara, daftar, qurS 'aw 'usTuwaana, kanza, kitaab, qalam, tuffaaHa, alkh*)

and imaginary money. Hang the store owner's sign above the store, for example,

دكان قيصر، متجر يوسف، محل نجوى.
(*dukkaan qaySar, matjar yoosuf, maHal najwa*).

Then trade roles and do the dialogue again.

Proverb

"عندما تحضر السوق تبيع وتشتري.
‘indama taHDar assooq tabee‘ watashtari.
When at the market, you buy and sell. "

Using the Arabic Alphabet

In each row connect the letters to form words. Write the words in the blank box.
Remember that the form of a letter may change, depending on its position in the word.

		اليمن	ن	م	ي	ل	ا	مثال Example
	ة	ي	د	و	ع	س	ل	ا	1.
	ت	ا	ر	ا	م	إ	ل	ا	2.
		ن	ي	ر	ح	ب	ل	ا	3.
			ن	ا	م	ع		4.
				ر	ط	ق		5.

Symtalk

J In the space, write the correct word or expression in Arabic.

.2 _____   .1 _____
                              _____

K Say the sentences, then write them in Arabic.

.1 _____

.2 _____

.3 _____

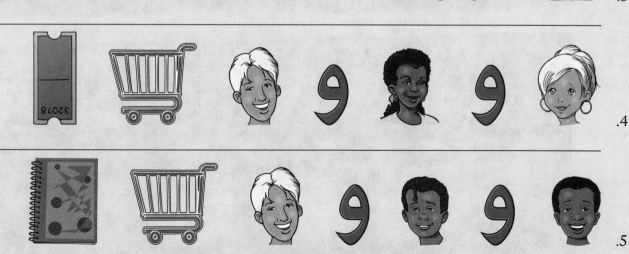

.4 _____

.5 _____

L **Work with a partner. Ask the question or give the answer. Then, write the dialogue.**

.1

_____   _____

.2

_____   _____

.3

_____   _____

.4

_____   _____

.5

_____   _____

M Look at the clippings to find the information requested below.

1. What are two items you can find at Shopping Center DEF?

   _____

   _____

2. How much money is each paper bill worth?

   _____

   _____

   _____

   _____

Unit 20

السفر والمواصلات

assafar wal-muwaaSalaat

Travel and Transportation

كيف تسافر؟
kayfa tusaafir?
How do you travel?

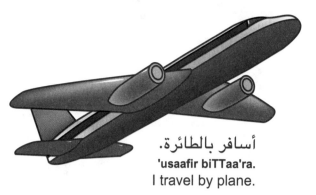

أسافر بالطائرة.
'usaafir biTTaa'ra.
I travel by plane.

أسافر بالسيّارة.
'usaafir bissayyaara.
I travel by car.

أسافر بالباخرة.
'usaafir bilbaakhira.
I travel by ship.

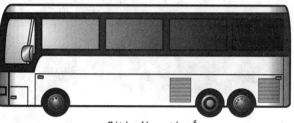

أسافر بالحافلة.
'usaafir bilHaafila.
I travel by bus.

أسافر بالقطار.
'usaafir bilqiTaar.
I travel by train.

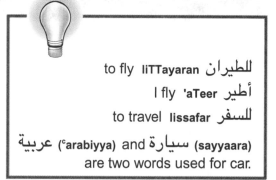

للطيران liTTayaran to fly
أطير 'aTeer I fly
للسفر lissafar to travel

عربية (°arabiyya) and سيارة (sayyaara)
are two words used for car.

في المطار
At the airport fil-maTaar

موظفة
muwaDHDHafa
clerk, agent

حقيبة / شنطة
Haqeeba / shanTa
suitcase

جواز سفر
jawaaz safar
passport

مسافر
musaafir
traveler

شباك التذاكر
shubbaakut-tadhaakir
ticket counter

الموظفة (f.): جوازسفرك، يا سيدي؟
Your passport, Sir? **almuwaDHDHafa: jawaaz safarak, yaa sayyidy?**

المسافر (m.): هو في حقيبتي، يا آنسة.
It is in my bag, Miss. **almusaafir: huwa fee Haqeebaty, yaa 'aanisa.**

الموظفة: من اللازم أن يكون بيدك... وخاصة في مكتب تأشيرات الدخول عند الوصول.
almuwaDHDHafa: minal-laazim 'an yakoon biyadik... wakhaaSatan fee maktab ta'sheeratud-dukhool °indal-wuSool. But you must have it on you... and especially at passport control upon arrival.

المسافر: حسنا. لحظة من فضلك. هذا هو! أين بوابة الدخول؟
almusaafir: Hasanan. laHDHa min faDlik. haadha huwa! 'ayna bawwaabatud-dukhool?
Okay. Wait, please. Here it is! And where do we board?

الموظفة: بوابة ٢٥ على يمينك. رحلة ممتعة!
almuwaDHDHafa: bawwaaba khamsa wa°ishreen °ala yameenak. riHla mumti°a!
At gate 25, on your right. Have a good trip!

المسافرة (f.): في أي وقت موعد القطار التالي إلى الأردن؟

At what time does the next train for Jordan leave, Sir?   almusaafira: fee 'ayy waqt maw°id alqiTaarut-taali 'ilal-'urdun?

الموظف (m.): عند الظهر يا سيدتي. هذا هو البرنامج.

At noon, Ma'am. Here's the schedule.   almuwaDHDHaf: °indaDH-DHuhr yaa sayyidati. haadha huwal-barnaamaj.

المسافرة: حسنا، أريد أن أشتري تذكرة ذهاب وإياب في الدرجة الثانية.

almusaafira: Hasanan, 'ureedu 'an 'ashtary tadhkarat dhihaab wa'iyyaab fid-darajath-thaaniya.
Good, then I'd like to buy a round-trip ticket in second class.

الموظف: هذه تذكرتك، ٧٥ ليرة من فضلك.

Here's the ticket. It's 75 pounds, please.   almuwaDHDHaf: haadhihi tidhkaratuki. khamsa wasab°een leera min faDlik.

السيد وليد (m.): المعذرة سيّدتي... كيف أصل إلى فندق رويسات؟

assayyid waleed: alma°dhara sayyidaty... kayfa 'aSil 'ila funduq ruwaysaat?
Excuse me Ma'am... how do I get to the Ruwaysat Hotel?

السيدة سمر (f.): إركب في حافلة رقم ٧ وإنزل عند مكتب البريد. الفندق على اليسار.

assayyida samar: 'irkab fee Haafila raqam sab°a wa'inzal °inda maktabil bareed. alfunduq °alal yasaar.
Take bus number 7 and get off at the post office. The hotel is on the left.

السيد وليد: شكرا سيدتي.

Thank you, Ma'am.   assayyid waleed: shukran, sayyidaty.

السيدة سمر: أهلا وسهلا بك يا سيدي.

You're welcome, Sir.   assiyyida samar: 'ahlan wasahlan bika, ya sayyidy.

Activities نشاطات

nashaaTaat

A **Match the Arabic on the right with the English on the left.**

A. a round-trip ticket

١. _____ إنتظر.
'intaDHir.

B. on the right

٢. _____ أحب.
'uHib.

C. Where do we board?

٣. _____ على اليسار.
ᶜalal-yasaar.

D. Here's the schedule.

٤. _____ إنزل عند مكتب البريد.
'inzal ᶜinda maktabil-bareed.

E. Get off at the post office.

٥. _____ أين بوابة الدخول؟
'ayna bawwaabatud-dukhool?

F. You must have it on you.

٦. _____ إركب الحافلة.
'irkab-alHaafila.

G. Wait.

٧. _____ تذكرة ذهاب وإياب.
tadhkara dhihab wa'iyyaab.

H. I would like....

٨. _____ من اللازم أن يكون بيدك.
minal-laazim 'an yakoon biyadik.

I. Take the bus.

٩. _____ هذا هو البرنامج.
haadha huwal-barnaamaj.

J. on the left

١٠. _____ على اليمين.
ᶜalal-yameen.

B **How do you travel? Complete each sentence in Arabic.**

١. أسافر بـ _____
'usaafir bi....

2. أسافر بـ ـــ.
'usaafir bi....

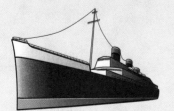

3. أسافر بـ ـــ.
'usaafir bi....

4. أسافر بـ ـــ.
'usaafir bi....

5. أسافر بـ ـــ.
'usaafir bi....

C Circle the correct answer.

1. Where do you go to take a train?

A. إلى المطار
'ilal-maTaar

B. إلى مكتب تأشيرات الجوازات
'ila maktab ta'sheerat-aljawaasaat

C. إلى المحطة
'ilal-maHaTTa

D. إلى الشارع
'ilash-shaariᶜ

2. What do you ask if you want directions to the train station?

A. أين بوابة الدخول؟
'ayna bawwaabatud-dukhool?

B. كيف أصل إلى محطة القطارات؟
kayfa 'aSil 'ila maHaTatil-qiTaaraat?

C. في أي وقت يترك القطار؟
fee 'ayy waqt yatruk alqiTaar?

D. كيف يمكنني مساعدتك؟
kayfa yumkinuni musaaᶜadatak?

3. What do you say when you want to buy a ticket?

A. هذا جواز سفري.
haadha jawaaz safari.

B. أحب شراء تذكرة سفر.
'uHibu sharaa' tadhkarat safar.

C. إلى أين أنت ذاهب؟
'ila 'ayn 'anta dhaahib?

D. كيف أصل إلى مكتب البريد؟
kayfa 'aSil 'ila maktabil-bareed?

4. If you don't want a first-class ticket, what do you say?

A. تذكرة ذهاب وإياب.
tadhkarat dhihaab wa'iyyaab.

B. محطة القطار.
maHaTTatul qiTaar.

C. حافلة رقم إثنين.
Haafila raqam 'ithnayn.

D. تذكرة درجة ثانية.
tadhkara daraja thaaniya.

الطقس جميل اليوم. سالي (.f) ومايا (.f) وميسم (.f) وجاد (.m) يريدون السفر بالقطار. هم

aTTaqs jameel alyawm. saali wamaaya wamaysam wajaad yureedoonas-safar bilqiTaar. hum

الآن على شباك التذاكر في محطة القطارات. سالي تشتري أربع تذاكر إلى

al'aan ᶜala shubbaakit-tadhaakir fee maHaTTatil-qiTaaraat. saali tashtari 'arbaᶜ tadhaakir 'ila

مجدلبعنا. أقارب سالي ومايا وميسم وجاد يعيشون في مجدلبعنا. هم الآن

majdalbaᶜna. aqaarib saali wamaaya wamaysam wajaad yaᶜeeshoon fee majdalbaᶜna. hum al'aan

ينتظرون القطار على رصيف رقم أربعة في محطة بحمدون. القطار يصل

yantaDHiroonal-qiTaar ᶜala raSeef raqam 'arbaᶜa fee maHaTTat bHamdoon. alqiTaar yaSil

إلى المحطة في الساعة الثانية بعد الظهر. جاد والبنات يصعدون إلى القطار. جاد

'ilal-maHaTTa fis-saaᶜath-thaaniya baᶜdaDH-DHuhr. Jaad walbanaat yaSᶜadoona 'ilal-qiTaar. jaad

يختار مقعد بجانب الشباك. سالي تجلس بجانبه. مايا تجلس على مقعد وراءه .

yakhtaar maqᶜad bijaanibish-shubbaak. saali tajlus bijaanibihi. maaya tajlus ᶜala maqᶜad waraa'ah.

وميسم تجلس على مقعد أمامه. في القطار الأولاد يتحدثون عن رحلتهم إلى

wamaysam tajlus ᶜala maqᶜad 'amaamah. fil-qiTaar al'awlaad yataHadathoona ᶜann riHlatihim 'ila

بحمدون. يصلون إلى مجدلبعنا في الساعة الثانية والنصف. في مجدلبعنا يأخذون

bHamdoon. yaSiloona 'ila majdalbaᶜna fis-saaᶜath-thaaniya wanniSf. fee majdalbaᶜna ya'khudhoona

الحافلة (الأوتوبيس) إلى بيت جدهم أبو هشام وجدتهم أم هشام.

alHaafila (al'ootoobees) 'ila bayt jaddihim 'aboo hishaam wajaddatihim 'umm hishaam.

seat	maqᶜad	مقعد	want to	yureedoon	يريدون
next to / beside	bijaanib	بجانب	they live	yaᶜeeshoon	يعيشون
behind him	waraa'hu	وراءه	they wait for	yantaDhiroon	ينتظرون
in front of him	amaamahu	أمامه	they get on	yaSᶜadoon	يصعدون
they take	ya'khudhoon	يأخذون	station / platform	raSeef	رصيف
relatives	aqaarib	أقارب	picks / chooses	yakhtaar	يختار

2. إلى أين يذهب الأولاد؟
'ila 'ayn yadhhabul-'awlaad?

1. أين الأولاد؟
'aynal-'awlaad?

ا. إلى راس المتن
'ila rasil-matn

ا. في المطار
fil-maTaar

ب. إلى مجدلبعنا
'ila majdalbaᶜna

ب. في الباخرة
fil-baakhira

ج. إلى صوفر
'ila Sawfar

ج. في التاكسي
fit-taaksi

د. إلى بسكنتا
'ila baskinta

د. في محطة القطارات
fee maHaTatil-qiTaaraat

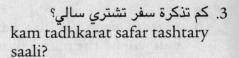

٣. كم تذكرة سفر تشتري سالي؟
kam tadhkarat safar tashtary saali?

أ. أربعة
'arbaᶜa

ب. واحدة
waaHida

ج. أربعة عشر
'arbaᶜta ᶜashar

د. إثنان
'ithnaan

٤. أين القطار؟
'aynal qiTaar?

أ. بجانب الشباك
bijaanibish shubaak

ب. مقعد وراءه
maqᶜad waraa'ah

ج. على رصيف رقم أربعة
ᶜala raSeef raqam 'arbaᶜa

د. مقعد أمامه
maqᶜad 'amaamah

٥. كيف يذهب الأولاد من محطة القطار في مجدلبعنا إلى بيت جدّهم؟
kayfa yadhhabul-'awlaad min maHaTTatil qiTaar fee majdalbaᶜna 'ila baytil-jaddihim?

أ. بالقطار
bilqiTaar

ب. بالحافلة
bilHaafila

ج. بالسيارة
bissayyaara

د. بالباخرة
bilbaakhira

E Complete the analogies.

١. موظف: _____ = مسافر: مسافرة

٢. طائرة: مطار = _____ : قطار

٣. باخرة: بحر = _____ : حافلة

٤. موظف: _____ = أستاذ: صف

٥. واحد: إثنان = _____ : أوّل

F لنتكلّم! (linatakallam!) Look at the pictures of a bus, an airplane, a car, a ship, and a train. Ask your speaking partner what each one is: ما هذا؟ (maa haadha?) He / she will answer. Then you get to ask him / her: كيف تسافر/ين؟ (kayfa tusaafir/tusaafireen?) as you point to a specific picture. He / she will answer again. Then switch roles.

G دورك! (*dawrak!*) With a partner act out the introductory dialogue, في الشارع . One of you will be the man asking directions and the other the woman helping him. This time, however, the man wants to go to another destination within the city. He will substitute another name for فندق الـ (i.e., إلى المتحف، إلى السينما، إلى السوق). The woman will recommend a different bus number. She will finish giving directions by saying that the place is on the right. Don't forget to say "Thank you" and "You're welcome!"

Proverb

في صحراء الحياة، العاقل يسافرُ مع
القوافل والمغفّل يسافرُ وحيداً.

fee SaHraa'il-Hayaat, al°aaqil yusaafiru
ma°il-qawaafil walmughaffal yusaafiru waHeedan.

In the desert of life, the wise person travels
with caravans and the fool travels alone.

Using the Arabic Alphabet

In each row connect the letters to form words. Write the words in the blank box.
Remember that the form of a letter may change, depending on its position in the word.

			مصر	ر	ص	م	مثال Example
		ن	ا	د	و	س	ل	أ	.1
		ل	ا	م	و	ص	ل	أ	.2
		ي	ت	و	ب	ي	ج	د	.3
		ر	ئ	ا	ز	ج	ل	أ	.4
		ب	ر	غ	م	ل	أ	.5
		س	ن	و	ت	.6
		ا	ب	ي	ي	ل	.7
ا	ي	ن	ا	ت	ي	ر	و	م	.8
ر	م	ق	ل	ا	ر	ز	ج	.9

Symtalk

In the space, write the correct word or expression in Arabic.

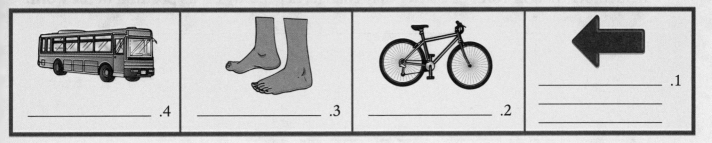

_____ .4   _____ .3   _____ .2   _____ .1
_____

I

Say the sentences, then write them. Express that each person is using their transportation to go to school.

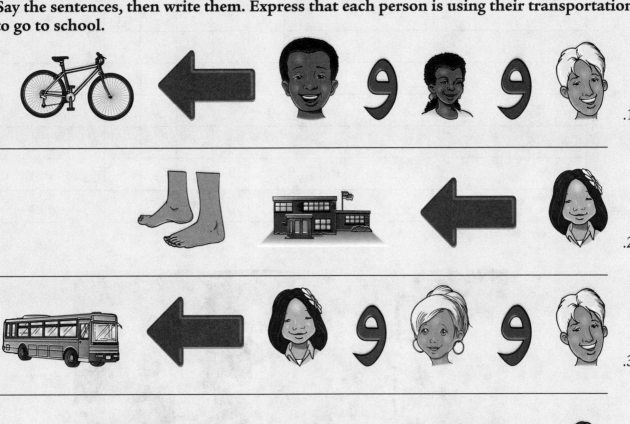

.1

.2

.3

.4

.5

Say and write a description of each scene in Arabic.

_____

_____

_____

_____

_____

.1

_____

_____

_____

_____

.2

_____

_____

_____

_____

.3

_____

_____

_____

_____

.4

من بيروت مباشرة مع

MEA

القوة التي تطمح لها..
الفعالية التي تحتاج لها

لقد حققت تويوتا من خلال تكنولوجيا المحرك المتعدد الصمام،
إنجازاً عظيماً آخر، يتمثل في الموازنة المثلى بين القوة والفعالية.
هذا الإنجاز الرائد يمكنك من تبديل السرعة بسلاسة وطواعية مميزين.
كما يؤمن لك توفيراً عملياً في إستهلاك الوقود.
التكنولوجيا لدى تويوتا.
تفتح أمامك آفاق جديدة في القيادة.

تويوتا

K **Look at the clippings to find the information requested below.**

1. The following could be a description of which advertisement, the one on the top or bottom? أسافر بالطائرة 'usaafir biTTaa'ira

_____

2. What is the message of the bottom clipping?

_____

_____